D1357523

PENGUIN BOOKS

HOW TO CHANGE EVERYTHING

HOW TO CHANGE EVERYTHING

The Young Human's Guide to Protecting the Planet and Each Other

NAOMI KLEIN

WITH REBECCA STEFOFF

PENGUIN BOOKS

PENGUIN BOOKS

UK | USA | Canada | Ireland | Australia
India | New Zealand | South Africa

Penguin Books is part of the Penguin Random House group of companies
whose addresses can be found at global.penguinrandomhouse.com.

www.penguin.co.uk
www.puffin.co.uk
www.ladybird.co.uk

First published in the USA by Atheneum Books for Young Readers,
an imprint of Simon & Schuster Children's Publishing Division,
and in Great Britain by Penguin Books 2021

001

Text copyright © Naomi Klein, 2021

The moral right of the author has been asserted

Interior design by Irene Metaxatos
The text for this book was set in Guardi LT Std

Printed and bound in Great Britain by Clays Ltd, Elcograf S.p.A.

The authorized representative in the EEA is Penguin Random House Ireland,
Morrison Chambers, 32 Nassau Street, Dublin D02 YH68

A CIP catalogue record for this book is available from the British Library

HARDBACK ISBN: 978–0–241–49291–8
INTERNATIONAL PAPERBACK ISBN: 978–0–241–49295–6

All correspondence to:
Penguin Books
Penguin Random House Children's
One Embassy Gardens, 8 Viaduct Gardens, London SW11 7BW

www.greenpenguin.co.uk

MIX
Paper from
responsible sources
FSC
www.fsc.org   FSC® C018179

Penguin Random House is committed to a
sustainable future for our business, our readers
and our planet. This book is made from Forest
Stewardship Council® certified paper.

In loving memory of Teo Surasky

(2002–2020)

—N. K.

CONTENTS

PART THREE

WHAT HAPPENS NEXT

CONCLUSION

AFTERWORD

INTRODUCTION
AT THE REEF

I spent a lot of time underwater as a kid. My father taught me to snorkel when I was six or seven, and those are some of my happiest memories. I was a shy child and often felt self-conscious. The one place where I never felt that way, where I always felt free, was in the water. Meeting ocean life so closely always amazed me.

When you first swim up to a reef, the fish mostly scatter. But if you hang out for a few minutes, breathing quietly through your air tube, you become part of the seascape to them. They'll swim right up to your mask, or gently nibble your arm. I always found these moments wonderfully dreamlike and peaceful.

So when I went to Australia for work years later, I decided to try to give my four-year-old son, Toma, the kind of undersea experience I had loved as a child. I wanted to show him that although the surface of the sea might look unremarkable, you can see a whole new and colorful world when you look beneath the surface.

Toma had just learned to swim, and we were about to embark on my first-ever visit to the Great Barrier Reef, the largest structure on Earth made up of living things—trillions of tiny coral creatures. The timing seemed perfect.

We went to the reef with a film crew and a team of scientists who had been studying the reef. I wasn't sure that Toma would be able to focus on the coral at all, but he had a flash of true wonder. He "saw Nemo." He saw a sea cucumber. I think he even saw a sea turtle.

That night, when I tucked him into bed in our hotel room, I said, "Today is the day when you discovered there is a secret world under the sea." He looked up, and the pure happiness on his face told me he understood. He said, "I saw it." I felt a mixture of joy and heartbreak, because I knew that just as he was discovering the beauty of our world, it was draining away.

You see, the Great Barrier Reef was the most stunning

place I had ever seen. It was a riot of life everywhere. Sea turtles and sharks swam past brilliantly colored coral and fish. But the reef was also the most frightening thing I had ever seen, because large parts of it—the parts I didn't show Toma—were dead or dying.

Those parts of the reef were a graveyard. As a journalist who had been reporting on climate change and the environment, among other subjects, I had come to the reef to write about it. I knew what was happening.

A reef-killing event called a mass bleaching had the Great Barrier Reef in its grip. Bleachings happen at times of high water temperature. The living corals turn ghostly and bone-white. They can return to normal if temperatures quickly go back down to lower levels. In the spring of 2016, though, temperatures had stayed high for several months. A quarter of the reef had died and turned into a brown goo of decay. At least another half of it had also been affected to some extent.

The water of the Pacific Ocean didn't have to warm very much to cause this massive die-off at the Great Barrier Reef. Ocean temperatures went up just 1.8 degrees Fahrenheit, or 1 degree Celsius, past the levels at which these corals can live. The dead and dying parts of the reef I saw were the result.

Corals are not the only things affected by bleachings

like the one I saw. Many species of fish and other creatures depend on coral for food or habitat. Food and
income for a billion or so people around the world come
from the fish that depend on coral reefs. When reefs die,
the loss reaches far. Sadly, more reefs are dying. That's
because temperatures are rising everywhere, not just at
the Great Barrier Reef, and these rising temperatures are
changing our world. This book is about that change. It

The vibrant undersea world of a healthy coral reef (left).

Coral bleached by warming water will die and turn brown if the water does not cool. And once a reef dies, its web of life will eventually collapse (above).

is about why temperatures are rising, how their rise is altering the climate and harming the planet we all share, and—most important—what we can all do about it.

What we can do goes far beyond making our individual efforts to reduce the pollution that's changing our climate. We do need to act against climate change to protect the natural world and the planet that supports all life, but we can go further than that.

Many things about climate change are unfair. One of them is the way it is stealing a healthy, clean planet from young people like my son, Toma. And from you.

It is also unfair that climate change affects people unevenly. Poorer communities, and minority communities, often suffer more than others from its effects. So this book is also about justice, or fairness. It is about how our response to climate change can help create not only a less polluted world but a more just one for all of us who share it.

You and your generation, and the generations yet to come, have done nothing to create the crisis of climate change, but you will live with the worst effects of it—unless we change things.

I wrote this book to show you that this change for the better *is* possible. Then, just as I was finishing the book, the world confronted a sudden, unexpected crisis. A new contagious disease known as a novel coronavirus appeared.

In early 2020 the virus grew into a pandemic, a disease that affected people in nearly every country. Rates of sickness and death were tragically high. Millions of people had to change their ways of life, staying home and avoiding other people, to slow the spread of the virus. Schools closed in many countries, throwing kids into a new routine of learning at home while missing their friends.

At the end of this book you'll find what I think we can learn from this shared worldwide experience. But as you read the following chapters, keep in mind that the coronavirus pandemic did not halt climate change—or the movement to bring climate change under control.

That movement is under way now. Its goal is to fight climate change while also making a fair and livable future possible for *everyone*. This is called climate justice. And young people are not just part of that movement. They are leading the way. Will you be one of them?

I hope this book will help you answer that question. It is meant to give you information and much more: inspiration, ideas, and tools for action.

First you'll see some of the steps that kids like you are taking against climate change and for social justice, including racial, gender, and economic justice. After that you'll dive into what we have learned about the state of the climate now, and how we got here. Then you can help decide what happens next. You won't be alone. In these pages you'll meet some of the young activists from all over the world who are working to protect our planet *and* win climate justice.

It can be scary to look closely at the realities of climate change, but don't let the facts overpower you. Remember that they are only part of the story. The rest of the story—the part of it that has fired up hundreds of thousands of young people like you in all parts of the world—is that we have choices. The huge uprisings against racism and for climate action show us that millions are hungry for change. We can build a better future, if we're willing to change everything.

PART ONE
WHERE WE ARE

CHAPTER 1
KIDS TAKE ACTION

They streamed out of their schools, bubbling with excitement. Little trickles of them flowed from side streets into grand avenues, where they mingled with other streams of children and teens. Chanting, chatting, dressed in everything from crisp school uniforms to leopard leggings, the kids formed rushing rivers in dozens of cities around the world. They marched by the hundreds, thousands, and tens of thousands.

Did businesspeople gaze down from their office windows and wonder what so many kids were doing out of school? Were shoppers puzzled by the surging excitement on the streets? Signs carried by the marchers answered those questions:

One of New York City's ten thousand young marchers was a girl who held up her painting of bumblebees, flowers, and jungle animals. The painting was lush, but the words with it were harsh: 45% OF INSECTS LOST TO CLIMATE CHANGE. 60% OF ANIMALS HAVE DISAPPEARED IN THE LAST 50 YEARS. At the center she had painted an hourglass running out of sand.

That day in March 2019 was the first global School Strike for Climate.

STUDENTS ON STRIKE

Organizers of the first school strike estimate that there were almost 2,100 youth climate strikes in 125 countries that day. More than a million and a half young people showed up. Most of them had walked out of school—

some with permission, some without—either for an hour or for a whole day.

Many of them took to the streets because they recognized a deep conflict in what they were learning about the world. Schoolbooks and documentaries had shown them ancient glaciers, dazzling coral reefs, and other living things that make up our planet's many marvels. But at almost the same time, they were finding out that much of this wonder has already disappeared because of climate change. Much more would be gone if they waited until they were grown up to do something.

Learning about climate change had convinced these kids that things could not continue on the same path. So, like many groups before them who had fought to transform the world, they took to marching.

But many of these young people went on strike not just to prevent losses in the future but because they were already *living* in a climate crisis. In Cape Town, South Africa, hundreds of young strikers chanted at their elected leaders to stop approving new projects that would contribute to our planet's warming. A year earlier, the huge city had come desperately close to running out of water, after several years of low rainfall and severe drought that were likely caused—or at least made worse—by climate change.

In the Pacific island nation of Vanuatu, young strikers yelled, "Raise your voice, not the sea level!" Their Pacific neighbor, the Solomon Islands, had already seen five small islands covered by the sea, which is rising as higher temperatures cause water to expand and glaciers and ice sheets to melt.

"You sold our future, just for profit!" the students in Delhi, India, yelled through white medical masks. Delhi often has some of the worst pollution in the world, in part because India is a major user of coal, a fuel that produces pollution. But the clouds of smog that form visible air pollution are not the only problem with coal. Burning

it also releases invisible substances called greenhouse gases into the air. And as the student marchers there knew, and as you will see, these gases are the reason our climate is changing.

Hope, determination, and a bouncing globe filled the air as young people filled the streets in Sydney, Australia, during the first School Strike for Climate.

That day was the first-ever worldwide climate strike—and it was created and run by kids. With that first school strike and those that have followed it, young people around the world are demanding a say in the future of their world.

"We Deserve Better"

One hundred and fifty thousand young people poured into the streets of Australia's cities for the first School Strike for Climate. They knew that climate change was already damaging their nation. One of its effects, as you saw at the beginning of this book, is that warming ocean water is killing the Great Barrier Reef, a natural treasure of Australia and the world.

Yet Australia remains a major producer and seller of coal. And coal, when burned as fuel to power electrical plants and for other uses, produces the greenhouse gases that drive temperatures higher. Fifteen-year-old Nosrat Fareha, an Australian strike organizer, said to the country's political class, "You have failed us all so terribly. We deserve better. Young people can't even vote but will have to live with the consequences of your inaction." Like other young people in other cities, Fareha was unafraid to speak the blunt truth to those in power. That fearlessness is one of the strengths of the youth movement for change.

A SCHOOLGIRL IN SWEDEN

The School Strike for Climate in March 2019 showed the world a youth movement that was large and growing. It had begun largely thanks to a fifteen-year-old girl in Stockholm, Sweden.

Greta Thunberg started learning about climate change when she was eight years old. She saw documentaries about melting glaciers and disappearing species. She learned that burning fossil fuels such as coal, oil, and natural gas emits—or releases—greenhouse gases into the atmosphere, and those gases contribute to climate change. Power plants, chimneys and smokestacks, cars, and planes all add greenhouse gas emissions to the air.

Meat-based diets also increase greenhouse gases, Greta learned. That's because raising livestock, especially cattle, means cutting down large amounts of forest to create grazing lands. This deforestation removes trees, and trees absorb the harmful greenhouse gas known as carbon dioxide, taking it out of the atmosphere. In addition, cattle and their manure add methane, another greenhouse gas, to the air.

As Greta grew older and learned more, she focused on scientists' predictions about what Earth will be like in 2040, 2060, and 2080 if humans do not change our ways. She thought about what this would mean to her own life—the disasters she would have to endure; the animals and plants that would disappear forever; the hardships in store for her own children, if she decided to become a parent.

But she also learned that the worst predictions of the climate scientists were not set in stone. By taking bold action now, humans can sharply increase the chances of a safe future. We can still save some of the glaciers. We can protect many island nations from being swallowed by the sea. We might avoid massive crop failures and unbearable heat that would send millions or even billions of people fleeing from their homes.

Why, Greta wondered, wasn't everyone talking about *preventing* climate disaster? Why weren't nations such as hers leading a dramatic charge to lower greenhouse gases? The world was on fire, yet everywhere Greta looked, people were still going about their lives, buying new cars and new clothes they didn't need, as though nothing were wrong.

At around the age of eleven, Greta fell into a deep depression. One reason she could not shake off her depression is that Greta has a form of autism that causes her to focus intently on subjects that interest her. So when Greta turned her laser-like attention to the climate breakdown, she saw and felt the full meaning of the crisis. She could not be distracted from it. Fear and grief for the planet overwhelmed her. Depression is complex, and there were other factors too. But it was impossible for Greta to understand why those in power were not doing much about the crisis of climate change. Weren't they also scared and angry?

A big part of coming out of her depression was finding ways to close the unbearable gap between what she had learned about the causes of the climate crisis and how she and her family lived. She convinced her parents to stop eating meat and to stop flying. The most important change for her, though, was finding a way to tell the rest of the world that it was time to stop pretending everything was fine. If she wanted powerful politicians to treat the fight against climate change as an emergency, she figured that her own life had to express that state of emergency too.

So in August 2018, at the age of fifteen, Greta didn't go to class when school started. Instead she went to

Sweden's center of government and sat outside with a handmade sign that read SCHOOL STRIKE FOR CLIMATE. She spent every Friday there, in her thrift-shop hoodie and light brown braids. This single action was the beginning of the Fridays for Future movement.

Greta Thunberg, a solitary Swedish schoolgirl, launched a movement that would reach every part of the world.

Public protest can be a powerful way to make a statement, but protest doesn't always make things happen overnight. At first people ignored Greta as she sat with her sign. Gradually, though, her protest got a bit of attention in the news. This caught the eyes of people who understood what she was trying to communicate, who agreed with her and also wanted to make a statement. Other students, and a few adults, started showing up with signs. Soon Greta was being asked to speak at climate rallies, then at United Nations climate conferences, and to the leaders of the

European Union, the British Parliament, and more.

Greta has said that people with her kind of autism "aren't very good at lying." She speaks in short, sharp truths. "You are failing us," she said to world leaders and diplomats at the United Nations in September 2019. "But the young people are starting to understand your betrayal. The eyes of all future generations are upon you. And if you choose to fail us, I say, we will never forgive you. We will not let you get away with this. Right here, right now is where we draw the line. The world is waking up. And change is coming, whether you like it or not."

Even if Greta's speeches brought no dramatic action from world leaders, her words electrified many others. People shared videos of her on social media. They talked about how she'd inspired them to face their own fears about the climate future and to take action. Suddenly children around the world took their cues from Greta. They organized their own student strikes. Many held up signs with her words: I WANT YOU TO PANIC. OUR HOUSE IS ON FIRE.

In December 2019, *Time* magazine named Greta Thunberg its youngest-ever Person of the Year for her activism in calling attention to the climate crisis. Yet she gives credit to other young activists who were *her* inspiration—students in Parkland, Florida. After seventeen people were murdered at their school in February 2018, Parkland students led a national wave of class walkouts for gun control. By following their example, Greta helped to bring the youth climate change movement to the world's stage, and by following her example, thousands more kids just like you have committed themselves to halting the dangerous progression of climate change.

Greta's Superpower

Living with autism isn't easy. For most people, says Greta, it "is an endless fight against schools, workplaces and bullies. But under the right circumstances, given the right adjustments, it *can* be a superpower."

And this is why Greta credits her autism for her clear vision of the problem and her power to speak clearly about it. "If the emissions have to stop, then we must stop the emissions," she says. "To me that is black or white. There are no gray areas when it comes to survival. Either we go on as a civilization or we don't. We have to change."

Learning about the ways our climate is changing

can lead to sadness, anger, or fear. But Greta discovered that she could help deal with those feelings by taking action and making a public stand—and when she did that, she became someone for many others to stand beside. Like the tiny piece of sand inside an oyster that causes a pearl to form around it, Greta's small act of protest helped create something beautiful and strong.

A LAWSUIT FOR CHILDREN'S RIGHTS

Young people are not just taking the climate movement to the streets. They are also taking it into the courts. Can they use international law to fight climate change? Sixteen kids from twelve countries on five continents are going to find out.

In September 2019 these climate activists, ranging from eight to seventeen years old, filed a legal complaint with the United Nations under an international treaty called the UN Convention on the Rights of the Child. This treaty took effect in 1989 to protect children's rights in the countries that signed it. It says, among other things, that every child has the "right to life" and that governments "shall ensure to the maximum extent possible the survival and development of the child."

The complaint singles out Argentina, Brazil, France,

Germany, and Turkey. Among the nations that have signed the UN treaty, those five produce the highest amounts of greenhouse gases. (The United States and China emit more greenhouse gases, but the United States has not signed the Convention on the Rights of the Child. China has not signed the part of it that would allow it to be sued.)

The sixteen young people who filed the complaint say that by not doing enough to limit or prepare for climate change, the five countries have failed in their duty to protect children's rights to life and health. It is the first UN climate complaint made on behalf of children around the world.

The next step will be for a committee of human-rights experts to review the complaint. This process could take several years. If the committee agrees with the children, it will make recommendations to the five countries on how they can meet their duty under the treaty. Although the committee does not have the power to force the countries to follow its recommendations, the countries that signed the treaty did pledge to live up to it.

The sixteen young activists are Greta Thunberg and Ellen-Anne of Sweden; Chiara Sacchi from Argentina; Catarina Lorenzo from Brazil; Iris Duquesne from France; Raina Ivanova from Germany; Ridhima Pandey from India; David Ackley III, Ranton Anjain, and Litokne

Kabua from the Marshall Islands; Deborah Adegbile from Nigeria; Carlos Manuel from Palau; Ayakha Melithafa from South Africa; Raslen Jbeili from Tunisia; and Carl Smith and Alexandria Villaseñor from the United States.

Catarina Lorenzo of Brazil spoke in September 2019 about a complaint filed at the United Nations by sixteen young people who accuse multiple countries of failing to act against climate change. Carlos Manuel of Palau (left) and David Ackley III of the Marshall Islands (right) were also among the sixteen.

David, Ranton, Litokne, and Carlos know firsthand that the need for action on climate change is urgent. They live on the island nations of the Marshall Islands and Palau in the Pacific Ocean. They are surrounded by dying reefs, rising seas, and ever more violent storms. Their message to the world is that even if people don't see climate change happening in their own home country or town, it *is* happening right now, and it will affect us all soon.

"Climate change is affecting the way I live," said Litokne in the complaint. "It has taken away my home, the land and the animals."

Carlos, from Palau, said, "I want bigger countries to know that us small island nations are the most vulnerable countries to be affected by climate change. Our homes are being slowly swallowed up by the ocean."

No matter what the committee of human-rights experts decides about this lawsuit, kids like you have shown that they are fierce and determined defenders of life on Earth. Other young people have followed their lead and filed similar climate-related lawsuits around the world.

Now that you've seen some of what young people are doing to call attention to the climate crisis, you may find yourself wondering what fueled their desire to act on such a large scale. The next chapters will give you a closer look at the climate crisis and its causes. You'll see what is driving so many kids like you to devote themselves to changing the world for the better.

CHAPTER 2

WORLD WARMERS

On Christmas Eve 2019, Antarctica got an unwanted gift—a new record. The ice-covered continent set a record for the most ice melted in a single day. Ice had turned to water on 15 percent of Antarctica's surface. But it hadn't been just one warm day.

December is summer in Antarctica, the melting season, because seasons in the southern half of the world are the opposite of those in the northern half. But even in summer, so much ice had never melted so quickly before. By Christmas, the summer meltwater level had been 230 percent higher than average for a month. Why? One scientist said that the continent had been "significantly warmer than average" all season.

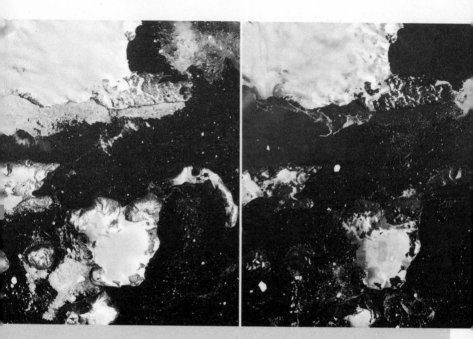

Photos taken just nine days apart in February 2020 show how much ice had melted at the tip of the Antarctic Peninsula after record high temperatures.

At the same time, far to the north, where December falls in winter, the Russian city of Moscow had a different, but related, problem: no snow.

For centuries, Moscow has been known for its winters. They are often bitterly cold, and snow usually falls before the end of the year. But in December 2019, temperatures were higher than normal. Gardens bloomed early. Children used ice rinks for soccer matches because there was no ice for hockey. City officials had to truck in tons of fake snow for a New Year's Day snowboarding event.

And while this fake snow piled up in Moscow, unusual warmth was leading to climate tragedy half a world away. On the last day of 2019, thousands of people in southeastern Australia fled to beaches to escape the flames that were tearing through their homes and communities.

Even though the southern summer was just getting started, already Australia was in the grip of yet another terrible heat wave. After three years with much less rain than usual, large areas were deep in drought. Trees and plants were bone-dry, ready to ignite. And they did. Small fires—started when lightning struck a dry tree or when people lit campfires, burned trash, or tossed cigarettes—quickly erupted into massive fires that sped through areas of dry vegetation. Plants were not the only things that burned, however. As happens with many wildfires around the world, homes, businesses, and other human-built structures were destroyed or damaged as well.

Perhaps the huge fires should not have been surprising. Just under a year earlier, Australia had started 2019 with its worst heat wave ever. In some places, temperatures had soared to above 104 degrees F (40 degrees C) for more than forty days in a row. Then, too, fires had wreaked havoc. They'd destroyed vast stretches of ancient forest in the Australian state of Tasmania, which had had the driest January ever recorded.

When 2019 ended, at least nine people in Australia had been killed by the fires. More than nine hundred homes had been destroyed, and more than 11 million acres (4.45 million hectares) of land had burned. Smoke and ash filled the air, darkening the skies even at noon. Tragically, about half a billion animals died because of the fires, including thousands of Australia's famous koala bears. Some rare animal species may well have been pushed into extinction. (It would get worse during the following year's fire season. By the end of March 2020, 34 people were dead, more than 3,500 homes destroyed, more than 46 million acres [18.62 million hectares] burned, and three billion animals killed, harmed, or displaced.)

Around the world, 2019 was a year of many such climate-related disasters and records.

In Asia, the highest-ever number of cyclones—fierce tropical storms—had torn through countries across the Indian Ocean. In the United States, floodwaters had covered large areas in the center of the country, destroying crops and driving people from their homes.

Heat records had been set across Europe and in Alaska. July 2019 was the hottest month on Earth since people had begun keeping records of temperatures. In September, the ice that has blanketed the Arctic Ocean for thousands of years (at least) shrank to the second-smallest area ever measured.

Almost a year later, Siberia—a traditionally cold region in northeastern Russia—was sweltering. In June 2020, temperatures hit 110.4 degrees F (38 C) in the remote town of Verkoyansk. This was the highest temperature ever recorded in the Arctic. Parts of Siberia were hotter than Florida, alarming scientists around the world—and also fueling hundreds of intense wildfires.

What did all these events have in common? Heat.

HEAT AND EXTREME WEATHER

Floods and droughts, heat waves and bitterly cold winter storms—how can heat cause so many different weather events? Heat waves are easy to understand. As temperatures rise, hotter days and nights become more likely, especially during summer or in places that are naturally warm. Hot nights are especially important. When temperatures fail to drop significantly at night, heat waves keep building without relief.

But heat also affects weather by changing the relationship between the Earth's surface and the atmosphere. As air heats up, it can hold more water vapor. Over land, warmer air draws more water out of soil through a process called evaporation, in which liquid becomes vapor—that is, gas. Water leaves plants through transpiration, a similar process. During a drought, increased evaporation and transpiration make the drought worse by drying out the soil and vegetation. The unusually dry vegetation, in turn, is at higher risk of burning in a wildfire.

Adding water vapor to the atmosphere intensifies other kinds of weather too. The extra moisture means that when rain or snow does fall, it is likely to be heavier than usual, causing floods or severe snowstorms.

Warmer air absorbs moisture from water as well as from land. As the atmosphere over the oceans grows warmer, it also grows wetter. One result of the warmer, wetter air over oceans, along with warmer water, is to make oceanic storms such as hurricanes, cyclones, and typhoons more powerful and destructive.

Increased heat also changes the behavior of the jet streams. These four fast-flowing air currents—one in each polar region and one on each side of the equator—occur where cold polar air meets warm tropical air. They usually move weather systems across the planet from west to east, but they can also twist or bulge south or north of their normal tracks. The cold Arctic region is heating up much faster than other parts of the world, which is likely weakening the northern polar jet stream, making it wavier. And as this polar jet stream twists southward, it carries frigid polar air and bitter winter weather with it. This helps explain why a planet that is getting hotter on average can still have extreme cold-weather events in some places.

And our planet *is* getting hotter. Sometimes this is called global warming, but "climate change" is a more useful term. That's because not every part of the world is warming all the time. The rising temperature of our planet is an overall average.

Heat waves and storms have always happened. So have cyclones, floods, and wildfires. Now, though, we know that the warming climate is fueling extreme conditions (such as drought) and extreme weather (such as megastorms). Climate change makes deadly, destructive natural events more likely.

But climate change isn't just about new weather records or numbers on a thermometer. The warming of the world also brings many smaller, creeping changes to plants and animals, oceans, and more. In this chapter you'll see what scientists have learned about the world's

A tornado left a trail of destruction in Joplin, Missouri, in May 2011. Climate change will likely make such extreme weather disasters more frequent and severe.

rising temperature and the changes that result. They are still working to fully understand these big and small changes, but the changes will touch the lives of all of us, and all life that shares our planet.

This is called climate disruption—climate change that disrupts, or breaks up, the way things have been all over the world. It brings new conditions that can be hugely destructive. The good news is that we know what is causing climate change. And because we have this knowledge, we also know what we can do to slow it down or stop it.

EARTH TODAY

Wherever in the world you live, you and other young people today have something in common. You are seeing climate disruption happen and worsen as you grow up.

During the twentieth century, the temperature across all the world's land and sea surfaces averaged 57.0 degrees Fahrenheit (13.9 degrees Celsius). In early 2020, the US National Oceanic and Atmospheric Administration (NOAA) reported that the global average temperature in 2019 had been 1.71°F (0.95°C) warmer than that. In fact, 2019 was Earth's second-warmest year on record, after only 2016. The twenty-first century is setting a lot of heat records. Nine out of the ten warmest years on record have happened since 2005, five of them since 2015.

You might not even notice if the temperature on a summer afternoon went up by less than one and a half degrees Fahrenheit, or less than a degree Celsius. So if Earth warmed by just that much in 2019, is it a big deal?

It is.

To raise Earth's average yearly surface temperature even a little bit takes a huge amount of heat, because the ocean can store a lot of heat energy before that energy affects the surface temperature. That's why a small rise in average surface temperature represents a big increase in stored heat. "That extra heat," says NOAA, "is driving regional and seasonal temperature extremes, reducing snow cover and sea ice, intensifying heavy rainfall, and changing habitat ranges for plants and animals—expanding some and shrinking others."

Greenland, for example, is a massive island between the Atlantic and Arctic Oceans. It is mostly covered by a thick ice sheet. Over a span of five days in the summer of 2019, Greenland's ice sheet lost fifty-five billion tons of water. The ice melted and flowed into the ocean. That was enough water to cover the state of Florida five inches deep! Scientists had not expected Greenland's ice to melt at that rate until 2070. Just a small change in temperature can have big consequences.

This is climate change and disruption in action. More than that—it is a call to climate *action*.

CLIMATE CHANGE BEFORE HUMANS—AND NOW

Climate change is our biggest challenge, but it is not new. The Earth's climate has changed many times. Around twenty thousand years ago, for example, much of the Northern Hemisphere was covered with ice sheets. We call this the Ice Age, but it was just the most recent ice age in the most recent geological period.

Over the last two million years, glaciers have formed in the northern reaches of the planet, then melted away, only to advance and retreat again and again. Because these vast glaciers held so much of Earth's water in the form of ice, sea levels dropped as much as 410 feet (125 meters) when the ice was at its peak, then rose again as the ice melted.

Earlier, during the time of the dinosaurs, Earth was much warmer than it is today. From 145.5 to 65.5 million years ago, there was little ice. Fossils show that warm-weather plants and animals thrived in the polar regions. And many scientists think that earlier still, before about 635 million years ago, our planet went through several periods of "Snowball Earth," or at least "Slushball Earth." It was blanketed with ice and snow, although open water may have remained near the equator.

Paleoclimatology—the science that deals with ancient climates—studies this history of past climate changes on Earth. Paleoclimatologists say that most of those changes have been caused by small shifts in Earth's orbit. These movements altered the way the sun's energy was distributed across the planet's surface. Some past climate changes, though, may have been caused by massive natural events here on Earth, such as eras of widespread volcanic eruption that went on for thousands or even millions of years. In addition to creating some of the rock and lava layers of the modern world, these eruptions filled the atmosphere with gases and particles, which also reduced the amount of heat energy at the planet's surface.

If climate change is part of our planet's history, what makes today's rising temperatures an emergency?

This time is different because of *us*.

Human civilization flowered after the last Ice Age ended. Everything about our lives is rooted in the conditions our species has known for the past twelve thousand years or so. Those conditions are changing rapidly. Keeping up with them will be the biggest challenge our civilization has faced.

But the key difference between today's climate crisis and the ancient climate changes is that *we* are causing this one. National Aeronautics and Space Administration (NASA) researchers report that much of the current warming trend, maybe all of it, is human-caused: "Most of it is extremely likely (greater than 95 percent probability) to be the result of human activity since the mid-20th century."

Our actions—burning fossil fuels, but also cutting down forests and raising a lot of livestock to eat—are changing the atmosphere in a way and at a speed that is outside its natural course. These activities of ours are adding greenhouse gases to the atmosphere.

A greenhouse is a building that traps and holds heat, so that people can grow flowers or fruits inside it even when the weather outside is too cold. Greenhouse gases work the same way, but on a global scale.

A lot of the heat energy that reaches Earth from the sun reflects off the planet and back into space. Certain gases in the atmosphere, though, trap some of that heat near the planet's surface. When those gases increase, more heat is kept, and temperatures go up. The rising temperatures, in turn, lead to the droughts, storms, wildfires, melts, and other features of our current climate crisis.

Our modern way of life is constantly emitting these heat-keeping greenhouse gases into the air. This means that we are constantly heating the planet in a way the Earth has never seen before.

You'll find out more about the links between human activity, energy use, greenhouse gases, and climate in chapter 4. First, though, you deserve to learn who is at greatest risk if we continue on our current path. You'll then see why this moment of danger is also a moment of great opportunity.

The bad news is that we are responsible for climate change. The good news is that we can do something about it. We already have the knowledge, tools, and technologies we need to do amazing things.

PREDICTING THE CLIMATE FUTURE

Scientists know that some climate disruption is going to happen no matter what we do, because warming that has already begun will not stop overnight. But we also know that if we do not act, climate change will be a lot worse. So climate scientists are constantly working on ways to measure our effect on the climate and to predict, or project, what the climate will be like in the future, to help us determine *how* to keep that warming to a minimum.

Climate scientists rely on two things: data and tools. The data is mountains of information. Over many years, measurements have been made of temperatures, wind speeds and directions, rainfall amounts, levels of salt in the oceans, sizes of glaciers, and much more. The tools are computer programs called models that are designed to mimic our planet's complex climate system. Researchers test a model by having it reproduce past changes in the climate, then comparing the results with the historical record. Next, they make predictions about the future, to show us what changes we can expect from specific changes in the climate system.

By changing the data that goes into a model, scientists can answer "what if?" questions. What if humans started reducing greenhouse gas emissions? What if they started emitting more? What role do clouds play in a given prediction? What if the amount of wildfire smoke increased every year?

Modeling is challenging because the climate system is so complex. Many programs for doing it exist, and they work in a variety of different ways. In addition, not all researchers use the same sets of data within these programs. This is why projections of the climate's future differ. Projections also change when scientists gather new data or create new, more precise models. When research showed that the oceans are warming faster than expected, for example, or that Greenland's ice is melting faster, that information changed many climate projections.

Two other things that can impact climate projections are tipping points and feedback loops.

Tipping Points:

The climate does not change in a steady, smooth line. Something that has been changing slowly can suddenly change quickly. This may happen because conditions have reached what is called a tipping point.

Imagine yourself slowly, steadily leaning to one side. At a certain point you will simply fall over. You have reached the tipping point. The remainder of your sideways movement will be swift and possibly catastrophic. And once you reach the point of falling, you cannot raise yourself back to your upright position.

The same thing can happen with climate change. For example, in 2014 scientists at NASA and the University of California in Irvine broke some disturbing news. They had been studying the West Antarctic Ice Sheet, part of the massive coat of ice that blankets the south polar continent. On an area the size of France, they said, glacier melt now "appears unstoppable." What had once been a slow flow of melt into the sea was significantly speeding up because the water where the glaciers meet the sea is getting warmer, melting them from beneath.

According to these researchers, a tipping point may have been reached, probably signaling the end of the West Antarctic Ice Sheet. If it keeps melting, as they predict, it will eventually raise sea levels some 9.8 to 16.4 feet (3 to 5 meters). "Such an event will displace millions of people worldwide," one of the scientists said.

While reaching a tipping point like this is serious, it still could take centuries for the ice sheet to collapse completely. Even if we can no longer completely prevent the disaster, we have time to delay it. The only way to do that is to slow the rate at which the ice sheets are melting and moving, which means slowing the warming of the planet. And the only way to do *that* is to cut the amount of the greenhouse gas emissions that are raising temperatures and fueling global warming.

Feedback Loops:

Another complication of climate projections is feedback loops. These happen when one process speeds up or slows down another process, and then the second process speeds up or slows down the first process, and on and on.

Sea ice shows us a feedback loop in action. Ice floats on water in the Arctic Ocean and on the edges of Antarctica. Warming temperatures cause some of it to melt in the summer. When it melts, a surface that was once covered by white ice is covered by dark water instead. White ice reflects the sun's heat away from the Earth's surface, but dark water absorbs heat. So when the warming trend melts some ice, there is less ice to reflect heat and more open water to absorb it. This boosts the warming trend, which now melts more ice faster. If nothing happens to break the loop, it will go on until the summers are ice-free.

Feedback also happens with permafrost, the soil that stays frozen year-round beneath the surface in cold places, such as high mountains and the polar regions. Permafrost contains material from things that were once alive, such as dead plants and bacteria. When temperatures rise high enough, permafrost starts to thaw, and that once-living

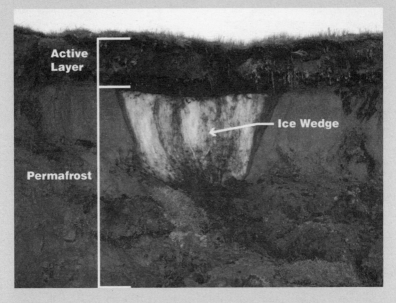

Active Layer

Ice Wedge

Permafrost

Permafrost (above) is permanently frozen soil—until temperatures rise, and it melts. A melting section of permafrost (right) has broken off into the sea.

material decays. This releases methane and carbon dioxide, two greenhouse gases. Putting more greenhouse gas into the atmosphere speeds up the warming, which speeds up the thawing . . . and another feedback loop is under way. Such loops add to the challenge of climate modeling because they cannot always be predicted.

All of this means that climate change is a fast-moving field of study, and scientists must keep developing new and more accurate tools for gathering data and modeling projections. These researchers are a vital source of information about what will happen to our

climate if we do nothing—and also about the changes we can make that will lead to better outcomes.

EARTH TOMORROW?

Scientists' climate models may produce a range of possibilities for the future, but many of them start at the same point in the past.

That starting point is the average world temperature in the late nineteenth century—around 1880. From that point, scientists measure the temperature today, then project future increases of 1.5°C (2.7°F), 2°C (3.6°F), and more.

Why those numbers? Because in 2016 nearly two hundred nations signed the Paris Agreement, part of the United Nations Framework Convention on Climate Change. The Paris Agreement set a goal of cutting greenhouse gas emissions to prevent the global temperature from increasing more than 2°C above preindustrial levels, but with efforts to keep the increase below the even better target of 1.5°C. These were believed to be the lowest targets that had a chance of being achieved.

The difference between 1.5°C and 2°C may seem small, but it means a lot. In September 2018, the Intergovernmental Panel on Climate Change (a large international team that the United Nations created in 1988 to provide the world with scientific information about human-caused climate change) published a report that compared the effects of 1.5°C of global warming to the effects of 2°C. The differences are huge.

At 2°C of warming, 1.7 billion *more* people would be at risk of severe heat waves one out of every five years than they would be at 1.5°C. Sea levels would rise by an additional four inches (ten centimeters). So for these reasons and more, 1.5°C of warming is a much better goal than 2°C.

How is the world doing on meeting that target?

At the time this book was written, the world had already warmed 1°C since the nineteenth century. The World Meteorological Organization, which tracks temperature, projects that we still are on a path to warming the world by 3°C (5.4°F) to 5°C (9°F) by the end of this century. And as we've already seen, 2019 was the second-warmest year on record. As this book was being finished, 2020 was on track to be in the top five.

Temperature isn't the only way to measure climate change, though. In November 2019, a NOAA report revealed that the global sea level had risen eight to nine inches (twenty-one to twenty-four centimeters) since 1880. For most of the twentieth century, the sea level rose at a rate of 0.06 inches (1.4 millimeters) a year. From 2006 to 2015, though, the ocean rose an average of 0.14 inches (3.6 millimeters) a year. This means the rise of the oceans is speeding up, just like the rise in temperature.

Why 1880?

The Baseline for Measuring Change

Most nations of the world have signed the Paris Agreement, which says that they will try to limit the planet's warming to 2°C (3.6°F) above preindustrial levels—or, better yet, to 1.5°C (2.7°F), if possible. But what does "preindustrial levels" mean?

The Paris Agreement doesn't define "preindustrial" precisely, but in general terms, it means "global temperature before the rise of modern industries powered by fossil fuels." As you'll see in chapter 4, that rise began around 1770, so the ideal baseline for measuring climate change would be the temperature of the world at that time.

Unfortunately, only a few good records exist of temperature measurements made before 1850. Scientists can estimate earlier temperature ranges from physical evidence, such as growth rings in trees and ice cores, long tubes of ancient ice carefully drilled from places such as Greenland and Antarctica. They can use computer models to estimate past temperatures based on things such as the position of Earth relative to the sun and the amount of ash and other particles in the atmosphere from volcanic eruptions. But for practical reasons, most climate models use the years 1850–1900 or 1880–1900 as their baseline, because that is when people began keeping reliable global temperature records.

Some amount of future warming is already locked in, so the sea will not stop rising entirely. In the worst case, if greenhouse gas emissions remain at their current levels, the sea level in 2100 could be as much as 8.2 feet (2.5 meters) higher than it was in 2000. This would flood huge areas of the world's low-lying coastlines and devastate dozens of major cities. It would turn millions, maybe billions, of people into climate refugees who would be forced to flee to new locations in other cities or even other countries.

Unless we do something about it.

NOAA projects that if humans reduce their emissions of greenhouse gases as much as possible to slow the warming of the planet and the melting of its ice, the global sea level in 2100 will likely be a foot (0.3 meters) higher than it was in 2000, instead of 8.2 feet (2.5 meters) higher. That is a huge difference, and it's why young people like Greta Thunberg are so frustrated that politicians aren't doing what is required to dramatically reduce the level of climate change.

Keeping the warming below 1.5°C, however, will be like turning an enormous ship around. The authors of the Intergovernmental Panel on Climate Change study found that it would mean cutting global carbon dioxide emissions almost in half by 2030, and bringing global emissions to zero by 2050. Not just in one country but in every major economy on the planet.

What would we have to do to cut emissions by that much? Carbon dioxide (CO_2) is the greenhouse gas that is doing the most to drive global warming. It is emitted when we burn wood, coal, oil, and gas. Deforestation, driving, flying, and many industrial activities such as drawing energy from fossil fuel–burning power plants all release carbon dioxide emissions.

Already the amount of CO_2 in the atmosphere is far past safe levels, so meeting the 1.5°C limit on warming would mean removing a great deal of it. This could be done through technology designed to capture and store carbon dioxide, but that technology has limits, as you will see in chapter 7. Or we could do it the old-fashioned way, by planting billions of trees and other plants. They draw CO_2 out of the atmosphere and add oxygen to it. Still, no one solution is quite enough on its own. The Intergovernmental Panel on Climate Change report says that to meet our targets, we need to make rapid "changes in all aspects of society."

We must decide to immediately change how our societies produce energy, how we grow our food, how we move ourselves around, and how our buildings are built. Among other possibilities, we could replace fossil fuels with clean, renewable energy sources such as wind and solar power, build networks of fast electric trains to take the place of some driving and flying, and design houses and office buildings that will require less energy to heat and cool.

But we need to think about deeper changes, too. We could use *less* energy, rather than just switching where we get it from. We could reduce the number of miles people drive by improving public transit, even making it free. And because every product we buy represents energy used at every step of making or shipping it (even "green" products!), we could all decide to shop less and consume less.

It is the biggest challenge we humans have faced. Are we up to it?

There is still time to reach that target of 1.5°C, but only if we act now.

IT'S NOT JUST THE HEAT

Warming is not the only factor stressing our planet. Many other human activities are changing the natural world, rapidly making it look very different from the beautiful and bountiful places you have all seen in nature documentaries about rain forests and oceans.

The difficult truth is that many of the life forms that share our planet are in a state of crisis. Some of them are losing their homes because human activity is filling in the wetlands, plowing the prairies, polluting water with chemicals and plastic, and smashing the reefs where they live. Some creatures are unable to adjust to the changing temperatures. Various bird species cannot find their seasonal foods, for example, because plants now flower before the birds return from migration. Other animals are being hunted toward extinction. And because humans have only begun to explore the deep ocean, whole species will be lost before we have even learned that they exist.

We are also cutting down trees at an alarming rate. People and corporations harvest trees for fuel, to make paper and other products, and to clear land for ranching cattle or growing plantations of cash crops such as corn, soybeans, and sugar.

Large stretches of forest on the Southeast Asian island of Borneo, for example, have been destroyed by the demand for palm oil, which is used in many foods, vitamins, beauty products, and other consumer goods. Natural habitat that was once home to countless plant and animal species has been replaced by rows of palm trees that can be harvested for this oil. In other places, such as vast areas of the Amazon rain forest, trees are cut down or deliberately set on fire to make room for cattle pastures.

Climate change worsens the effects of these bad choices. For example, forests that are already under threat of human deforestation are also dying more rapidly as tree-destroying insects move into new territories that have grown warmer because of climate change. And, of course, this creates a feedback loop of warming, because when trees die, they stop drawing CO_2 out of the atmosphere. Dead trees are also drier than living ones. They are more likely to catch fire.

Our actions don't just hurt the planet, the environment, and other living things, though. They harm us, too, and not always in ways that are easy to see. One example is the effect of carbon dioxide on our food.

Scientists have discovered that when the amount of CO_2 in the atmosphere goes up, the nutritional quality of food crops goes down. In experiments, researchers surrounded open-air plots of rice and wheat with machines that added CO_2 to the air. The grains of those plants had lower than normal levels of protein, iron, zinc, and some B vitamins.

If greenhouse gases keep increasing, our food crops may become less nutritious overall, adding to problems of hunger and disease. Even more serious, if climate change continues on its current path, heat and drought could also make it impossible to farm large areas of food-producing land.

All of us can do things in our daily lives to slow down climate change and ensure that this doesn't happen. We could follow Greta Thunberg's example and convince our families to give up meat and airplane travel. Even two meatless days a week, or one less flight per year, is a start. But while our individual choices make a difference, individuals alone cannot bring about the sweeping changes we need. If we are to make those changes, then government, business, and industry—including the major sources of greenhouse gases—must also make very different choices.

This is the knowledge that drove young climate activists into the streets. This is why it is so important for us to join together and make our voices heard, telling our leaders that we care passionately about the future and helping to shape a better way forward. Now that you know what those climate activists know, this book will show you how you can get involved too.

Because by speaking up together to say no to rising temperatures, we also say yes to a more fair and equal world.

CHAPTER 3

CLIMATE AND JUSTICE

Not everyone experiences the effects of climate change to the same degree. We live in a world of racial, economic, and climate injustice, with some people having far more than they need and many others not having close to enough. This chapter will show you how these injustices began and how they are often interconnected—and also some of the ways people are working to end them.

HURRICANE KATRINA: AN UNNATURAL DISASTER

I went to the city of New Orleans, Louisiana, after the

Hurricane Katrina storm struck the US coast of the Gulf of Mexico in August 2005. A day before Katrina made landfall in Louisiana it was a Category 5 hurricane and the strongest storm ever measured in the Gulf of Mexico at that time. Fortunately, it weakened the next day. Katrina reached the coast of Louisiana as a Category 3 hurricane. Still, it devastated portions of the state's coastline with wind, rain, and high seas, and it unleashed floods in New Orleans, a metropolitan area with a population of 1.3 million.

A couple of weeks later I went with a team to New Orleans to document how the still partly flooded city was coping after the storm. Everyone was supposed to be off the streets by six o'clock in the evening, but as the curfew drew close, we found ourselves driving in circles, unable to find our way. The traffic lights were out, and half the street signs had been blown over or twisted sideways by the wind. Water and debris made it impossible to drive along many roads.

Events such as Hurricane Katrina are often called natural disasters because they involve some event in the natural world: a storm, an earthquake, a flood. But just as with climate change, there was nothing natural about the disaster we witnessed in New Orleans. Although Katrina had started as a devastating hurri-

Hurricane Katrina turned New Orleans into an obstacle course of downed electrical wires and debris.

cane, it had lost most of its strength by the time it reached the city. It should never have devastated the city as it did.

What went wrong? The answer once again lies with human decisions.

A Weakened City:

When Katrina arrived, New Orleans's flood defenses failed. The city was surrounded by a series of levees between it and the nearby Mississippi River and two large lakes. The levees, which are long structures similar to dams, were supposed to protect the city from high water in storms like Katrina. But in spite of many warnings over a period of years, the levees had fallen into disrepair, and the government agencies responsible for them had left them that way. Why? Because the neighborhoods most at risk if the levees failed were those that housed poor Black people, who had little political power.

So when Katrina hit and the floodwaters poured over and through the broken levees, the sharp divide between the haves and have-nots of New Orleans suddenly appeared in the world news. People with money drove out of town, checked into hotels, and called their insurance companies. The 120,000 people in New Orleans who did not have cars counted on the government to get them out of the flooded city. While they waited for aid that did not come, they made desperate HELP signals on their roofs and used refrigerator doors as rafts. In too many cases, the help did not come, and more than a thousand people lost their lives.

Images of the city's distress shocked the world. Many people had grown used to the fact that health care and good schools were not distributed equally in the richest nation on Earth, but disaster responses were supposed to be different. People took it for granted that the government—at least in a rich country—would help all people during a disaster. New Orleans showed that that was not the case. The city's poorest residents, who were overwhelmingly African American, were largely left to fend for themselves.

People helped each other as best they could. They rescued each other in canoes and rowboats. They emptied their refrigerators and fed each other. And when food and water ran out, they took supplies from stores. The media painted these desperate Black citizens as "looters" who would soon invade and disrupt the dry parts of the city, which were mostly inhabited by white people. Police checkpoints were set up to trap the Black citizens in the flooded zone. Police officers at one point shot some Black residents on sight, then later falsely claimed that these unarmed people had fired on an officer. White vigilantes came into the city with guns, proudly declaring, "You loot, we shoot."

I saw firsthand how jumpy the police, soldiers, and private security contractors still were when I arrived. Many of them had arrived in New Orleans fresh from war zones in Iraq and Afghanistan. They seemed to be under orders to treat the city's residents as if they were enemies, not people in need of their help. Even the National Guard, when they finally arrived to get people out of the city, were often needlessly aggressive. They pointed machine guns at people who were boarding buses. They separated many children from their parents.

The levees of New Orleans had been neglected at least in part because most of the residents they were supposed to protect were poor people of color. But the failure to keep the levees in good shape was also part of a larger pattern across the country. The nation's infrastructure—that is, public structures built and maintained by the government, such as roads, bridges, water systems, and levees—was being neglected. The neglect grew out of the way the US government had come to treat its responsibility to the public.

"Shrink the Government":

Not everyone agrees on what the government's role should be, or how far it should reach into the lives of citizens. For decades, many of the world's economic and political decisions have been defined by three interrelated principles that aim to reduce the role of government. Together these principles are sometimes called neoliberalism.

The first principle is deregulation—or undoing the rules and regulations that limit what privately owned banks and industries can do to make profits. The second is privatization, which means turning over to for-profit companies services that were once paid for and operated by the government, including schools and highways. The third principle is a goal of low taxes, especially for corporations and the wealthy. And without the money collected from taxes, governments have less money to spend on things like infrastructure, which is part of the reason the levees of New Orleans had been neglected.

These principles are all based on the idea that businesses should be as free as possible so that they can grow, sell more products, earn more profits, and create more jobs. They're also based on the idea that government should be run more like a business, and be less involved in guaranteeing that people's basic needs are met.

Long before Hurricane Katrina, this "shrink the government" view had been in direct conflict with the idea of the "public good"—the belief that there is value in doing things that support and benefit *all* members of society, even when there isn't a profit to be made. The "shrink the government" outlook was an attempt to undo the belief that all of us have the same rights to a decent life, one that includes such things as parks, good public education, and a well-maintained infrastructure. Support in government for the public good had weakened, which helps explain why the levees of New Orleans were so close to the breaking point when Hurricane Katrina landed.

But the physical infrastructure was not the only thing that failed because of this outlook. So did the human systems of disaster response.

All levels of government in the United States have agencies whose job is to help people get out of harm's way when a disaster is coming, and to provide shelter, medical care, and other relief afterward. The Federal Emergency Management Agency (FEMA) oversees these efforts on a national level. After Katrina, FEMA badly failed the people who were stranded in flooded New Orleans.

It took five days for them just to get food and water to twenty-three thousand people who had taken emergency shelter in a sports arena called the Superdome. Reports of the miserable conditions under the dome shocked the world. One reason for FEMA's failures in New Orleans was that many of the agency's officials had little or no experience with disaster management. They had received their jobs because of their political loyalty. Also, as part of the move to run government more like a business, those people who did have years of experience in the agency had been replaced by newcomers with less seniority and experience.

Another reason for FEMA's failures was that the agency had not stockpiled enough emergency supplies.

The same thing would happen across the nation in 2020, when the need for personal protective equipment to battle the coronavirus crisis in hospitals was met with empty shelves, showing the shortcomings of both the federal government's preparations and a health-care and hospital system based on making the biggest possible profits. In such a system, an empty hospital bed or a well-stocked supply warehouse is regarded as a business failure, because it represents money that is not being made or money that has been spent. The bed and supplies would be sensible preparations for disaster, but because the system is under pressure to make money rather than spend it, such preparations do not get made, and people will suffer when that disaster comes.

In New Orleans in 2005, local leaders such as the mayor also contributed to this problem by delaying orders for citizens to evacuate the city and by failing to arrange for food, water, and medical supplies in emergency shelters. The failure of both federal and local officials to spend effort and money on preparing to care for the public good in the event of a severe storm made the problem much worse.

For a few weeks, the flooded streets of New Orleans called attention to these economic policies that had made Katrina worse than it had to be—an unnatural disaster on the heels of a climate one. But as much as I had been shocked by what I'd seen during the flood, what happened next shocked me even more.

THE POOR SUFFER FIRST AND WORST

After Hurricane Katrina flooded New Orleans, corporations and their representatives jumped at the chance to take advantage of the tragedy.

Families had fled or been bused out of New Orleans and ended up all over the country. A leading economist of the "smaller government" school called the scattering of the city's schoolchildren "an opportunity to radically reform the educational system." His idea of reform was privatization. He called for the public schools to be reopened as private schools. In this case, some of the schools might no longer be free or might have different educational standards than public schools.

One Republican congressman from Louisiana said afterward, "We finally cleaned up public housing in New Orleans" and gave God credit for destroying these poor neighborhoods. But the destruction of some neighborhoods had been done purposefully, and not by the hurricane. In the months after the storm, with New Orleans's poor and Black residents conveniently out of the way, officials did not work on helping people return to their homes. Instead, thousands of the public housing units where the displaced residents had lived were destroyed— but not always because of storm damage. Many of these buildings stood on high ground and had suffered little or not at all from Katrina. They were "cleaned up" not by the storm but by wrecking crews. Condos and town houses replaced them. These new homes were far too expensive for most of the people who had lived in those neighborhoods before the storm, but they enriched the real estate developers who had built them.

With the city still reeling, plans such as this took shape on a wish list of things corporations wanted. These things were supposedly meant to rebuild the city. But instead of aiding the people who had been harmed by the disaster, or repairing the infrastructure to protect them in the future, corporations pushed for changes that would weaken labor laws, environmental regulations, and public schools. What did they strengthen? The oil and gas industry, the real estate industry, and other business interests. That is because corporations and companies exist primarily to make profits. From a business point of view, even a disaster can become a moneymaking opportunity.

This approach to "recovery" from Katrina brought more examples of injustice. Many of the private companies and contractors that swarmed the city seeking to profit from the disaster took large payments of government money but delivered poor service, or sometimes no service, in return. This was possible because there was almost no government oversight of how money was spent or where it went. (When you keep shrinking the government, that's what happens.)

One company received $5.2 million to build a base camp for emergency workers, a vitally important task. But the camp was never completed. The company that had received that government contract turned out to be a religious group. Its director admitted, "About the closest thing I have done to this is just organize a youth camp with my church."

After the tragedy, the government could have done things that would have helped rebuild the city and also helped local people put their lives back together. It could have required its contractors to hire local people at decent wages. But officials did not do that. Instead, the local people had to watch as contractors brought in underpaid workers, including many immigrants, to do work that made fortunes for the contractors. Even worse, after the work was done, many of these immigrant workers then faced being deported from the country.

New Orleans's poor people were already at a social and economic disadvantage before Katrina destroyed their homes, jobs, and communities. Then the storm made their circumstances much worse. The right kind of help during the disaster relief and rebuilding could have done something to correct these inequalities. The opposite happened instead. Then, a few months after the storm, Congress decided to cut $40 billion from the federal budget, to make up for the billions of dollars it had given to private companies in the form of contracts and tax breaks. What did Congress cut to save money? Student loans, food stamps, and health-care benefits for the poor, among other programs.

The fact that the poorest citizens in the country paid more than once for the big contractor bonanza after Hurricane Katrina is a major example of climate injustice. They had already paid a high cost when disaster had affected their communities more than other parts of the city. Then they paid again when relief turned into handouts to corporations. And, finally, they paid again when the few programs that directly helped unemployed and working poor people across the nation were gutted to pay for those handouts.

Katrina showed how our current economic system views disasters and other extreme events such as wars. This is "disaster capitalism"—when the rich and powerful take advantage of painful shocks to widen existing inequalities instead of correcting them. The rich and powerful see these tragedies as chances to seize control and change things in ways that favor banks, industry, and powerful politicians, not ordinary people.

Disasters *are* opportunities for change because they disrupt normal life. In a state of emergency, ordinary laws and practices may be suspended. People feel desperate and confused. They may be so concerned with survival or recovery that they cannot focus on the large questions of what is being done, and who is benefiting.

In the era of climate change, as natural disasters become more frequent, this deeply unjust pattern continues to repeat itself after storms, floods, and fires. The pattern can also be clearly seen across all the harm caused by climate change. All too often it is the disadvantaged—the poor, people of color, and Indigenous Peoples—who are hurt first and worst.

This is why the movement to stop climate change must be a movement for social and economic justice as well. And it is why we must learn to turn disasters into opportunities to make *positive* changes for everyone, not just a few. We must shift away from using each crisis to help the business interests, which often contribute most to climate change, because this response to disasters creates a dangerous feedback loop. Our efforts and our government's spending should instead go directly toward helping the people who have been harmed, rekindling the once powerful belief in the public good.

"Why Not Try to Help?"

At the age of twenty-one, Elizabeth Wanjiru Wathuti created a movement to help fight climate change and economic injustice in Kenya, in eastern Africa. Her tools to accomplish this are shovels and trees—and the young people she inspires.

"I'm passionate about the environment because I was lucky enough to be able to connect with nature when I was young, and as long as I can remember I was angered by environmental injustices whenever I saw them, like people cutting down trees and polluting our rivers," she told the environmental group Greenpeace. "So I thought to myself, why not try to help other young people be more conscious of the environment?"

Wathuti grew up in a forested region of Kenya. She planted a tree there when she was seven. That was her first piece of climate activism, but it would not be her last. She drew inspiration from another Kenyan woman, Wangari Maathai (1940–2011), who launched the Green Belt Movement to teach

Kenyan women about the benefits of planting trees to protect the environments of their homes, schools, and churches. The Green Belt Movement led to similar movements in other countries, and Maathai helped women plant some twenty million trees across Africa. She eventually received a Nobel Peace Prize for this work. Now Wathuti is carrying on the tree-planting tradition, with a focus on helping children become environmental activists.

In 2016, Wathuti founded the Green Generation Initiative to help children appreciate and plant trees. In three years, her organization planted more than thirty thousand trees. Wathuti happily reported in 2019 that more than 99 percent of those trees have survived.

With her team of forty young volunteers, Wathuti's Green Generation Initiative has worked with more than twenty thousand schoolchildren. Her success shows the power kids like you can have when given a way to take positive action. An act as simple as planting a tree can grow into a revolutionary movement.

"I envision a world where we can all live in harmony with nature without harming the planet," Wathuti says. "A world where everybody is mindful of how they will leave the planet for future generations, and a world where people and planet are put before profit."

NEW ENERGY FOR THE NORTHERN CHEYENNE

Five years after I saw the impact of Katrina in New Orleans, I witnessed a different response to climate change and injustice on the Northern Cheyenne Reservation in southeastern Montana. When I first visited the reservation, the community was under a cloud. The cloud was not a weather problem, though, but a conflict over coal.

The Threat of Coal:

The rolling hills of this region are dotted with cattle, horses, and striking sandstone rock outcrops—and beneath many of those hills sits a whole lot of coal. The mining industry wanted to get at the coal under and near the Northern Cheyenne Reservation. It intended to build a railroad to take the coal out of the area, to be sent to China and other parts of the world. This mine and railroad, though, could threaten the safety of a key water source, the Tongue River. In addition, the railroad would likely affect the Native burial grounds of the Cheyenne.

The Northern Cheyenne had been fighting off the mining companies since the early 1970s. But in 2010, the region was in a fossil-fuel frenzy. At that time, nearly half of the power used in the country came from burning coal, and the industry was eager to export the fuel to other countries. Worldwide, the demand for coal was expected to increase by more than 50 percent in just twenty years.

It wasn't clear how long the anti-coal voices in the Northern Cheyenne community would be able to hold these companies off. The anti-coal forces had just lost an important vote at the State Land Board about this new mine. It was to be built at Otter Creek, just outside the Northern Cheyenne Reservation, and it was the biggest new coal mine being planned in the United States.

After losing the vote on the mine, activists had turned their attention to opposing the Tongue River Railroad. Without the new railroad, there would be no hope of getting the coal out—which meant there would be no point in building the new mine. The Cheyenne, though, had not united against the railroad. It seemed likely that both the railroad and the mine might go ahead.

"There is so much going on, people don't know what to fight," Alexis Bonogofsky told me. Her job at the time was with the National Wildlife Federation, supporting Indigenous tribes in their use of their legal rights to protect the land, air, and water. She worked closely with the

Northern Cheyenne, who had a proud history of using the law to protect the land.

Decades earlier the Northern Cheyenne had argued that their right to enjoy a traditional way of life—guaranteed by their treaty with the United States—included the right to breathe clean air. The federal Environmental Protection Agency (EPA) agreed. In 1977 it gave the Northern Cheyenne Reservation the highest possible class designation for air quality. This let the tribe go to court against polluting projects that threatened the quality of their air. The tribe argued that pollution from as far away as Wyoming violated its treaty rights, because the pollution could travel to the reservation and possibly damage its air and water quality.

But the Otter Creek mine and the Tongue River Railroad were proving harder to fight. Pressure came from within the tribe as well as from the mining industry. The Northern Cheyenne had recently elected a former coal miner as tribal president. He was determined to open up reservation lands to the companies that wanted to extract—or remove—their resources.

Some other Northern Cheyenne were also tempted by the mine project. It represented money that the community badly needed. Unemployment was high. Poverty and substance abuse were ravaging the reservation.

People's desperation made them willing to listen when the mining companies came in and promised jobs and money for new social programs.

"People say . . . if we go ahead and do this, we can have good schools, a good waste system," said Charlene Alden, the tough and tireless director of the tribe's environmental protection offices. It was getting harder to find voices in the community willing to speak out against coal mining. She worried that sacrificing the health of the tribe's land for coal dollars would push the Cheyenne further away from their culture and traditions. In the end, this could mean more depression and substance abuse, not less.

"In Cheyenne, the word for water is the same as the word for life," Alden explained. "We know that if we start messing around too much with coal, it destroys life."

It already was. Many houses on the reservation had been built from government kits in the 1940s and 1950s. They were terribly drafty. In the cold winter months, people blasted the heat in their homes, but it flew out through cracks in the walls, windows, and doors. On average, people paid $400 a month for heat, which came from one of two fossil fuels, either coal or propane—a type of gas. Some people, though, paid more than $1,000 each month. To make matters worse, the fossil-fuel energy sources added to the climate crisis that was already hitting the region with long droughts and massive wildfires.

So the only way to break the deadlock, Alden believed, was to show the next generation of Cheyenne leaders a different path out of poverty and hopelessness, one that would not cost them the land of their ancestors. She saw many possibilities. One of them involved heat and straw.

A nonprofit organization had come to the reservation a few years earlier to build a handful of model homes. The homes were made with straw bales, which is an ancient method that keeps buildings warm in winter and cool in summer. Alden said that the families in those homes had heating bills of "$19 a month instead of $400."

But why did the tribe need outsiders to build homes based on Indigenous knowledge? Why not train tribal members to design and build them, and get funding to do it across the reservation? There would be a green-building boom, and the trained builders could then use their skills in other places, so that more homes could be built without ravaging the land.

But such a program would take money, which the Northern Cheyenne did not have. People had hoped that President Barack Obama would increase funding for green—or environment-friendly—jobs in disadvantaged communities. This would have helped fight both climate change and poverty, but most of those plans were set aside after the United States had an economic crisis that began in 2008. Still, Alexis Bonogofsky and Charlene Alden wanted to show the Northern Cheyenne that they had possibilities other than coal. They set to work.

A year after my first visit to the reservation, Bonogofsky called to tell me that she and Alden had scraped together some money from the EPA and the National Wildlife Federation. They were launching an exciting new project: solar-powered heaters. Did I want to come back to Montana to see it and tell people about it?

Absolutely.

The Promise of Sunlight:

My return trip to the reservation could not have been more different from the first, in both weather and spirit. It was spring. Tiny yellow wildflowers and bright green grass covered the gentle hills. Fifteen people had gathered on the lawn in front of a house. They were there to learn how a simple box made mostly of dark glass could capture enough heat to warm the whole house.

Their teacher was Henry Red Cloud of the Lakota people. He had built his first wind turbine, a machine that captures wind power to make electricity, out of parts from a rusting truck. Later he won awards for bringing wind and solar power to the Pine Ridge Reservation in South Dakota.

Now he had come to teach these Northern Cheyenne youth how to install solar heaters on their reservation homes. The heaters were worth $2,000 each but were being installed for free, thanks to the funds Bonogofsky and Alden had gathered. The devices would cut heating costs in reservation homes by as much as half.

Red Cloud wove his technical lessons about the solar heaters together with thoughts about how "solar power was always part of Natives' lives. . . . It ties in with our culture, our ceremony, our language, our songs." He showed the trainees how to use a tool called a Solar Pathfinder to find where the sun would hit each side of the house every day of the year, because the solar boxes need at least six hours of sunlight a day to work well. For a few houses that were nestled too tightly against trees or mountains for the boxes to be used, Red Cloud reasoned that solar roof panels might be used on them instead, or another renewable power source.

One of the last houses to get a solar heater was on a busy street in downtown Lame Deer, the small town at the center of the reservation. As Red Cloud's students measured, drilled, and hammered, they started to draw a crowd. Kids gathered to watch the action. Old women asked what was going on. "Half the cost of electricity?" they said. "How do I get one?"

Henry Red Cloud (center) and his solar warriors install solar panels, a step toward green, renewable energy—and environmental justice.

Red Cloud smiled. This is how he builds a solar revolution on Indigenous lands—not by telling people what they should do but by showing them what they *can* do. Several of those first students took more training with Red Cloud. Others joined them. He was teaching them, he told them, not just to be technicians but to be "solar warriors," fighting for a way of living grounded in gratitude and respect for the Earth.

In the months and years that followed, the fight against the Otter Creek mine and the Tongue River coal train sprang back to life. And suddenly there was no shortage of Cheyenne to hold protests. They demanded meetings with government officials and made passionate speeches at hearings. Red Cloud's solar warriors were front and center, wearing red "Beyond Coal" T-shirts.

Vanessa Braided Hair was one of Red Cloud's star students and also a volunteer firefighter. In the summer of 2012 she'd battled a fire that had burned more than ninety square miles (230 square kilometers) of land. It had destroyed nineteen homes on the Northern Cheyenne Reservation alone.

So Braided Hair did not need anyone to tell her that we are in a climate crisis. She had seen it. She welcomed the chance to be part of the solution to climate change—but it went deeper than that. As Red Cloud had said, solar power fit with the worldview in which she had been raised. "You don't take and take and take. . . . You take what you need and then you put back into the land," she said.

Another of Red Cloud's students, Lucas King, spoke to coal company representatives at a hearing about Otter Creek. "This is Cheyenne country. It has been for a long time, longer than any dollar has ever lasted. . . . Please go back and tell whoever you have to that we don't want [coal development]. It's not for us. Thank you."

The solar warriors and other Cheyenne kept resisting the railroad and mine plans. So did people outside the reservation. Students from the University of Montana started a movement they called the Blue Skies Campaign to help organize protests in neighborhoods along the rail lines that already existed. The students knew that in many such towns, coal trains are run through poor neighborhoods, choking them with coal dust and the fumes of diesel fuel. Blue Skies held protests, organized marches, and went to city council meetings to urge action against existing and new rail lines and fossil-fuel developments.

In August 2012, people sat on the steps of the state capitol for five days to protest the state's leasing of land to oil companies. Two years later, fifteen hundred people from a dozen Montana communities held a statewide day of action for clean energy. In 2015, when the Northern Cheyenne Tribal Council held a vote about the Tongue River Railroad, not a single vote supported the railroad.

With grassroots activism blocking the railroad, there would be no new mine at Otter Creek. Yet larger forces worked against the mine too. Coal's time as an energy superstar was drawing to an end. The market for coal began to lose strength as more and more people woke up to its problems, which included dangerous work in mines as well as pollution and greenhouse gas emissions. Demands for clean, green, renewable energy grew louder. Coal mines in the United States began closing, and plans for new ones fell through. In early 2016, the company behind the Otter Creek mine and the Tongue River Railroad went bankrupt.

Green, renewable energy is far better for all of us than fossil fuels. But building renewable energy projects is also an opportunity to right the injustices that many Native People still suffer. That means doing these projects with the active participation and consent of the Native Peoples who live nearby, and for their benefit. Unlike the residents of New Orleans, who were shut out of jobs in the recovery work after Katrina, Native People must take part in the projects that are built on their lands, as with Red Cloud's solar boxes, so that skills, jobs, and money flow to their communities.

The Cheyenne show us that shifting from mining coal to building wind and solar farms can and should be more than just flipping a switch from dirty underground power to clean aboveground power. It can also set right old injustices. The best way for a green-energy revolution to succeed is to involve and lift up communities, not just corporations. That's how you build an army of solar warriors.

SACRIFICE ZONES

The burning of fossil fuels is the biggest driver of climate change. But even if fossil fuels didn't heat the planet, it would still be worth switching to clean, renewable power like the solar heaters on the Northern Cheyenne Reservation. The communities that live close to where fossil fuels are extracted, processed, transported, and burned know that these fuels are unhealthy for people as well as for the planet.

Depending on fossil fuels to power our lives means sacrificing people and places. To extract these fuels, people's healthy lungs and bodies must be sacrificed to the bad air and the dangerous work of coal mining. People's lands and water are also sacrificed to damage from mining, drilling, and oil spills.

Just fifty years ago, scientists giving advice to the United States government spoke of the possibility of "national sacrifice areas." Some began to say that it was necessary to let certain people and regions suffer harm in order to benefit the country as a whole. One such zone is Appalachia, a region of the eastern United States, from northern Georgia and Alabama to southern New York.

Appalachia has long been known for two things: beautiful mountain scenery, and coal. Now, in too many parts of the region, the first thing has largely been sacrificed for the second. Mining companies have blasted away entire mountaintops, occasionally displacing whole towns. They have dumped the waste into valleys and streams, simply because that type of mining is cheaper than digging underground.

For a government or society to be willing to sacrifice whole regions and communities in this way, it must see those people as set apart somehow, and less valuable than other citizens. Stereotypes are developed that cast hardworking people in these regions as somehow less than others. Then those stereotypes become the excuse for not protecting those communities from harm. That's what happened to the Black residents of New Orleans, before and after Hurricane Katrina. And it happened in Appalachia, too. People from there used to be insultingly called "hillbillies." Stereotypes portrayed them as ignorant, drunk, and lawless. And that stereotype served a profitable purpose: once someone has defined you as a "hillbilly," who cares about protecting your hills?

It happens in cities, too. North America's power plants and oil refineries, which create noise and pollution, are overwhelmingly located next to Black and Latinx communities. Companies put them there because they believed that poor people would not have the political or economic power to demand better treatment—unlike wealthier areas, which often get the attention of politicians because the people who live in them can afford to make political donations and hire lobbyists to promote their interests in state capitals and in Washington, DC. That inequality in power is why people of color have been forced to carry the poisonous burden of our economy's reliance on fossil fuels. This is known as environmental racism.

For a very long time, the sacrifice zones of the world had certain things in common. They were places where poor people lived. Out-of-the-way places. Places where people had little or no political power, usually because of their race, their language, or their social class. And the people who lived in these places knew they had been written off.

But the sacrifice zones are now getting bigger. Coal may be on the way out, but our hunger for energy has led the mining industry to invent new ways of getting oil and gas out of the Earth. One way is hydraulic fracturing, also known as fracking. Liquid forced into the ground under high pressure fractures—or breaks—the rock. Then the natural gas or oil trapped within the rock can be pumped out. Although fracking carries the dangers of leaks, fires, water contamination, and making the ground unstable, companies consider the sacrifice worth it if they can sell the fuel at a profit.

Fracking and other new techniques have begun to pull fossil fuels from sites where it was once too difficult and costly for the industry to reach the fuels. Oil and gas under the deep ocean, for instance, or mixed into beds of shale or sand became much more feasible to extract. These new technologies created a huge boom in fossil fuels, which only kept the problem of greenhouse gases alive in a new way.

And all that fuel has to move. In the United States alone, the number of railcars carrying oil rose from 9,500 to almost half a million between 2008 and 2014. More oil spilled from US trains in 2013 than in the forty years before combined. After a fall in oil prices and a shift to more oil being moved through pipelines, less oil is traveling by train now in the United States, but millions of people still live in the path of poorly maintained "oil bomb" train lines. In July 2013, a train with seventy-two cars full of oil exploded. As a result, half of the downtown of Lac-Mégantic, a small town in Quebec, Canada, was flattened. Forty-seven people died.

An investigation by the *Wall Street Journal* newspaper in 2013 found that more than fifteen million Americans lived within one mile of a well that had been recently drilled or fracked—a well that could potentially be the source of an oil or gas leak or a fire. "Energy companies have fracked wells on church property, school grounds and in gated developments," wrote journalist Suzanne Goldenberg in another newspaper, the *Guardian*.

In 2019, the administration of President Donald Trump said it would now allow fracking on the borders of some of America's national parks—something oil companies had dreamed of for a long time. In Great Britain, the areas being considered for fracking add up to about half the entire island.

No place, it seems, is safe from being sacrificed if fossil fuels can be extracted from it. Our sacrifice zones are getting wider and wider. And as you know, the pollution, waste, and destruction caused by extracting coal, oil, and gas from the Earth are only part of the problem. The other part is the greenhouse gases that enter Earth's atmosphere when those fuels are eventually burned. They are driving climate change, and climate change threatens everyone and every part of the world.

We are all in the sacrifice zone now, unless we join together and raise our voices in opposition.

CLIMATE CRUELTY

When the first global School Strike for Climate came to the city of Christchurch, New Zealand, kids of all ages poured out of their schools in the middle of the day. As in New York and dozens of other cities around the world, the young people waved signs as they merged into larger streams. By early afternoon, two thousand of them were gathered in a square at the city's center to listen to speeches and music.

"I was so proud of the whole of Christchurch. All of these people had been so brave. It isn't so easy to walk out," Mia Sutherland told me. She was seventeen years old and one of the organizers of the strike.

The high point, Sutherland said, was when the entire crowd sang a strike anthem called "Rise Up." The song had been written by twelve-year-old Lucy Gray, who'd been the first to call for the student climate strike in Christchurch.

Sutherland is an outdoorsy person. She had started to worry about climate disruption when she'd realized that it would harm not just far-off places but also parts of the natural world she knew and loved. Then she learned that entire Pacific nations are at risk because of sea level rise and the growing power of cyclones. That's when climate change went from an environmental issue to a human-rights issue for her. "Here in New Zealand we are part of the Pacific Island family," she said. "These are our neighbors."

On the climate strike stage in Christchurch, young people took turns speaking at the microphone. "Everyone looked so happy," Sutherland later recalled. Then, just as she was about to speak, a friend gave her a tug and said, "You have to shut it down. Now!"

A police officer walked onto the stage, took the microphone, and told everyone to leave the square. As Sutherland went to catch a bus, she saw a headline on her phone. A shooting had just taken place ten minutes away from where she was standing. She was stunned.

She soon learned that at the very same time as the students' climate strike, an Australian man living in New Zealand had driven to the Al Noor mosque, one of the Muslim houses of worship in Christchurch. He'd walked inside and opened fire on the worshippers as they'd prayed. Six minutes later he had driven to another mosque and continued his massacre. More than fifty people died as a result of the shootings. Nearly as many were seriously injured.

The Christchurch killer was a white supremacist, someone who believes that whites are better than people of other races and should have more rights and privileges. He was driven by racist hate. What he wrote about his crimes makes it seem that ecological breakdown was one of the things that fed his hate.

The killer called himself an "eco-fascist." The green-sounding "eco" comes from "ecology," the study of how living things relate to each other and to their environment. "Fascist" comes from "fascism," a political viewpoint that favors authoritarian, dictatorial leadership above democracy and favors racial or national identity above individual human rights. Letting non-white immigrants into places like New Zealand and Europe, the killer wrote, was "environmental warfare" because it would overpopulate and destroy those regions.

This is false. It is the richest parts of the world and the very richest people that have polluted our planet most. But as our societies start to tackle the ecological and climate crisis, this kind of white-power eco-fascism could become more common. In fact, governments of some majority-white countries, even countries that have not taken many steps to fight climate change, are already using the climate crisis as an excuse to keep out immigrants and to cut back on aid to poorer nations.

The governments of the European Union, the United States, Canada, and Australia have already made it much harder to enter their countries as immigrants. Increasingly these governments are locking up migrants in camps and prisons. This, they claim, will prevent other desperate people from seeking safety by crossing their borders.

This is one example of climate *injustice*, because one of the reasons people are forced to move and emigrate is the impact of climate change. Another example of climate injustice is the way some of the world's super-rich are already taking steps to protect themselves from the worst effects of climate change and social upheaval. They are building well-stocked, well-guarded private ranches or mansions that are really fortresses. This deepens the divide between the haves and the have-nots, further eroding the ideas of a shared fate and the public good. It also hoards resources that could be used to help others. Wealth and private security guards, however, cannot shield anyone forever from drastic upheavals if the worst projections of climate change come to pass.

All of this is why we cannot think about climate action without thinking about justice and fairness at the same time. Because right now, many responses to climate disruption are clearly *un*fair. The people who polluted the least are suffering the most. And the people who polluted the most are using their money to protect themselves from the worst results of their actions.

So humanity faces a choice.

In the rough and rocky future that has already begun, what kind of people are we going to be? Will we share what's left and join together to halt the threat that is advancing on all of us? Or will we try to hoard what's left, look after only "our own," and lock everyone else out?

PAYING OUR CLIMATE DEBT

We are not fated to go down the path of climate cruelty. There are other paths for the future, if we choose to take them. We could start down them by being honest about what the richer, overdeveloped parts of the world owe to the poorer, underdeveloped ones: a climate debt.

Greenhouse gases build up in Earth's atmosphere over time. Carbon dioxide (CO_2), for example, stays in the atmosphere for several hundred years—some of it even longer. Our planet's climate is changing today because of more than two centuries of built-up emissions. Countries that have powered their industrial economies with fossil fuels for a long time have therefore done much more to raise the planet's temperature than countries that came later to industry. And, as chapter 4 of this book will make clear, much of the wealth of these rich parts of the world has its roots in people stolen from Africa and lands stolen from Indigenous Peoples.

This means that the climate crisis was overwhelmingly created by the world's wealthiest countries, including the United States, the nations of western Europe,

Russia, Great Britain, Japan, Canada, and Australia. With less than one fifth of the world's population, they have emitted nearly two-thirds of the carbon dioxide that is now changing the climate. The United States alone now emits about 15 percent of the world's carbon, even though it has less than 5 percent of the world's population.

But even though the wealthier countries and people are responsible for most of the climate crisis, they are not the most vulnerable to its effects. Few of the richest nations are located in the hottest and driest parts of the world, and all of them are able to produce what they need, or can afford to import it—at least for now.

In addition, although Australia and western North America have been ravaged by droughts and fires, the higher overall incomes and living standards in these countries mean that many people have refrigeration and air-conditioning and can move to new homes if necessary. Of course, this is not true for an ever-growing number of people in these countries.

As with the aftereffects of Hurricane Katrina, the poorest people and nations are hurt first and worst by greenhouse gas emissions. In 2018, the World Bank estimated that by the year 2050, flooding, heat, drought, or food shortages caused by climate change will drive more than 140 million people from their homes in South Asia, Latin America, and Africa south of the Sahara Desert. Many experts think the number will be even higher. Most of these displaced people will stay in their own countries, crowding into cities and slums that are already overcrowded and stressed. Many, though, will try for a better life elsewhere.

Basic justice says that victims of a crisis caused by others are owed something. So a vital step toward justice would be for the world's wealthiest to lower their greenhouse gas emissions, as much and as quickly as they can. Another step would be to recognize that all people have the right to move and seek safety when their land is too parched to grow crops or is threatened by fast-rising seas. This could involve helping climate migrants move to new locations within their countries or welcoming them to other countries.

A third step would be for the richer, more developed parts of the world to pay their climate debt to the poor, less developed nations. The idea behind climate debt is that the richer countries owe something to the poorer countries because of their history.

Earth's atmosphere can safely absorb only a limited amount of carbon dioxide. This is called the "carbon budget." Wealthy countries had already used up most of the planet's carbon budget before most poorer ones had a chance to industrialize. The reasons for this are complex, but they have to do with the legacies of colonialism and slavery. Now these lower-income countries are trying to catch up. Their people want many of the things that people in wealthier countries take for granted: electricity, sanitation, and convenient transportation networks. And they have a right to them. But the trouble is this: if everyone in the world copies the wasteful, fossil-fuel-burning lifestyles that are common in rich nations, the planet's temperature will soar.

The idea of climate debt is a way of finding a fair solution to this dilemma. Starting in 2006, the relatively poor South American nation of Ecuador tried to show the world how this solution could work—but few were willing to listen at the time.

Yasuní National Park in Ecuador is an extraordinary stretch of rain forest. Several Indigenous tribes that live in the park have rejected all contact with the outside world in order to protect their way of life. This means that they have little immunity to common diseases such as influenza and could be at great risk if forced into contact with outsiders.

The park is also home to a vast diversity of plants and animals. As many tree species grow in just 2.5 acres (1

Protesting oil development in Ecuador's Yasuní National Park, the park's Indigenous People came face-to-face with officers in the capital city of Quito.

hectare) of the park, for example, as are native to all of North America. It is also home to many threatened animal species, like the giant otter, the white-bellied spider monkey, and the jaguar. Yasuní is the kind of place that David Attenborough makes those amazing documentaries about!

But underneath that riot of life sits oil—up to 850 million barrels of it. The oil is worth billions, and oil companies want to get at it. If they did, it would bring a lot of investment to Ecuador's economy. That money could be used to fight poverty. On the down side, burning all that oil, and logging the rain forest to get it, would add 547 million tons of carbon dioxide to the atmosphere. This is a problem for everyone on Earth, including the people of Ecuador.

In 2006, an idea was put forth by an Ecuadorian environmental group called Acción Ecológica (Ecological Action). The government of Ecuador would agree not to allow drilling in Yasuní. In return, the other countries of the world would support that decision by paying Ecuador part of the money it would lose by leaving the oil in the ground.

This arrangement would be good for everyone. It would keep planet-warming gases out of our atmosphere. It would also protect the rich biological diversity of Yasuní. And it would raise money for Ecuador to invest in health, education, and clean, renewable energy.

The point of this plan was that Ecuador should not carry the whole burden of leaving its oil in the ground. The burden should be shared by the highly industrialized countries that have already put most of the excess carbon dioxide into the atmosphere—and have grown wealthy doing it (with the help of slavery and colonialism, as you'll see in the next chapter). Under the plan, the money Ecuador received could be used to help the country move to a new era of green development, leapfrogging over the dirtier model that has prevailed for centuries. The Yasuní plan would be a model for paying the climate or ecological debt in other countries.

The government of Ecuador championed the Yasuní plan to the world. The people of Ecuador strongly supported it. A poll in 2011 showed that 83 percent of them wanted to leave Yasuní's oil in the ground. This was up from 41 percent just three years earlier, showing that a plan for positive change can capture people's imaginations quickly.

A goal of $3.6 billion for Ecuador was set to protect Yasuní from drilling. But contributions from developed countries were slow to arrive—or never did. After six years, only $13 million had been raised.

So, because the plan had failed to raise the hoped-for payments, in 2013 the president of Ecuador said that he was going to allow drilling. Ecuadorian supporters of the climate debt plan did not give up. Citizens' groups and nonprofit organizations campaigned against drilling. Protesters stood up to arrests and rubber bullets. Yet in spite of their efforts, drilling began in Yasuní in 2016. Three years later the government allowed drilling in a third oil field inside the park, this time in the area where tribes had lived without contact with the outside world.

Ecuador's government says that the oil extraction is being done with great care to protect the environment. But even if this is so, drilling in Yasuní means more use of fossil fuels, more greenhouse gas emitted into the atmosphere, and more climate change.

Latin America, Africa, and Asia are filled with opportunities for the richer parts of the world to step up and pay their climate debts. For that to happen, the wealthy peoples and nations of the world must acknowledge what they owe to the countries that find themselves in a crisis they did little to create.

What are the responsibilities of the rich? What are the rights of the poor, no matter where they live in the world? Until we face these questions, we will not have a worldwide approach to climate change that is big enough to solve the problem. And we will keep having more heartbreaking lost opportunities like in Yasuní.

LABORATORIES FOR THE FUTURE

After Hurricane Katrina, New Orleans became a kind of laboratory. Like mad scientists, corporations and their supporters in government and in think tanks carried out experiments on the public body. They tinkered with turning areas that had once been part of the common good, such as public health and education, into business opportunities. In the end, they left the city even more starkly divided between the wealthy and the poor, and weakened for the next disaster.

But future disasters *could* become laboratories for the common good. Disasters—whether events such as floods, earthquakes, and storms or political upheavals such as wars—often highlight inequality, as Katrina did in New Orleans. Social and climate injustice become easier to see. But disasters also disrupt ordinary life. Often they push people to come up with new ways of doing things. This is where disaster becomes opportunity.

In the wake of many disasters, the rich and powerful have seized the opportunity to become richer and more powerful. What if, instead, disasters were turned into opportunities to empower and strengthen the public good?

Government, local officials, and aid groups could allow and encourage people to react to disasters in ways that help each other and also help local communities, not just the corporations that are rich enough to weather the storms. Chapter 6 tells about a few places where this has already happened. That is the path of climate justice, and it lowers the chances that we will all be battered by the storms ahead. And this path is achievable.

As you've seen in part 1, today's young climate protesters are right—the current state of the climate and our society puts us at a critical decision point. How will we shape the future through our actions, not just as individuals but as societies and as a species?

To avoid repeating the mistakes of the past, we need to know how we got to the present moment of global climate crisis and how we built up that climate debt. As you will see in the next chapter, that story also begins in a laboratory.

PART TWO
HOW WE GOT HERE

CHAPTER 4

BURNING THE PAST, COOKING THE FUTURE

limate change was born in 1757 in a laboratory, or a workshop. The place was a bit of both. It belonged to a twenty-one-year-old Scotsman named James Watt.

Watt's craft was making and repairing the delicate instruments used by scientists and mathematicians. After he fixed some astronomical equipment belonging to the University of Glasgow, he was invited to open a shop within the university. Six years later, the university asked him to repair an engine. That repair job would eventually lead James Watt to a new power source—a steam engine that a historian named Barbara Freese called "perhaps the most important invention in the creation of the modern world."

The engine led to the rapid growth and spread of industry, then to the large-scale burning of fossil fuels in order to power industry—and, in time, to the climate crisis.

WATT POWER

We've talked a lot about fossil fuels, but what exactly are they? Coal, oil, and natural gas are called fossil fuels because they are made of the remains of living things that died millions or even hundreds of millions of years ago. These living things were not towering dinosaurs like those you may see in museums. Instead, coal and some types of natural gas come from the remains of long-dead trees and other plants. Oil and most natural gas come from the bodies of tiny water plants like algae, or microscopic ocean-dwelling creatures called plankton.

When these living things died, they sank to the bottoms of ancient swamps and seas. Through ages of time, earth steadily built up over the trillions and trillions of remains. Pressure from the weight of the earth created chemical reactions that turned the organic remains into coal, crude oil, or natural gas.

People used fossil fuels long before James Watt. In

places that had wetlands and bogs, people dug blocks of peat out of the ground. Peat is ancient plant matter that is partly decayed. If left in the ground for a few more tens of millions of years, it could have become coal. Even dug out as peat, though, it was still burned to heat houses.

Coal was buried deeper in the ground than peat, and it was harder to get, but it burned hotter. By Watt's time, coal-burning fireplaces or furnaces heated many British homes. In fact, the machine that Watt was asked to repair in 1763 was a Newcomen engine—an early steam engine, invented in 1712 by Thomas Newcomen, that was used mainly to pump water out of flooded coal mines.

At its simplest, a steam engine is something like a large teakettle. Only, instead of whistling out into your kitchen, the steam from the boiling water is trapped and used to power a machine. Just as a teakettle needs to be heated on a stove, a steam engine cannot heat water without energy from some kind of fuel.

Newcomen engines burned coal. The burning coal heated water in a container called a boiler, turning it into steam. The steam flowed into a sealed chamber with a tight-fitting moving part called a piston. The pressure of the steam pushed the piston, and the energy of the moving piston operated rods attached outside the chamber.

The moving rods could drive a pump that would remove the water from a mine that had flooded.

When Watt repaired the university's Newcomen engine, he saw that it was not very efficient. It wasted energy because the engine cooled at each stroke of the piston, meaning that the steam had to be constantly reheated. Several years later, Watt figured out how to redesign the steam engine. His version would be more efficient and vastly more powerful.

It took years for Watt to perfect his design and find the right partner to help him turn it into a business, but in 1776 the new engine was put to work. Its first job was powering the pumps that drew water out of flooded mines, as Newcomen's engine had done.

Watt's partner, Matthew Boulton, pointed out that the market for mine-draining pumps was limited, but many other kinds of work also needed power. At Boulton's urging, Watt went on to invent a version of his engine that could power machines beyond pumps. In 1782 a sawmill ordered one of the new engines. The mill had been using twelve horses to provide energy to the machines that cut timber. Watt calculated that the work done by one horse was equal to lifting thirty-three thousand pounds a distance of one foot in one min-ute. (This is the origin of the horsepower unit of energy

By making modern industry possible, the steam engine—and the machines it powered, such as this train—changed the world. They also started changing its climate.

measurement.) His engine replaced all twelve horses.

James Watt did not invent the steam engine, but he changed it in a big way. Strong and tireless, his engine ate coal from what seemed like a limitless supply, then churned out energy. It was the perfect machine for the way powerful people of Watt's time and place had come to view the Earth and our relationship to it.

A WORLD FOR THE TAKING

Have you ever tried to describe your relationship with nature? Do you think it is pretty much the same as your society's relationship with the natural world, or do you have ideas that don't match what you see around you?

Humans have had many ways of thinking about their lives in the natural world. For example, the Haudenosaunee people (sometimes called Iroquois) have an ancient philosophy that calls for every decision to be evaluated based on its impact not just on generations alive today but seven generations into the future. Many cultures have philosophies that teach their members to be good ancestors as well as good citizens, doing nothing that would prevent future generations from having good lives. And as we heard from young people living on the Northern Cheyenne Reservation, their culture teaches them to take no more than they need, and to give back to the land, so that it can continue to renew itself and support life.

These systems of living still exist among some groups, especially among Indigenous Peoples around the world. In much of the modern world, though, those systems gave way hundreds of years ago to a different view of the relationship between people and nature. People began to see nature as an object or a machine, something humans can and should control. From the sixteenth century on, this view took hold in Europe and its colonies, including what would become the United States. It is woven into our global economy, which values taking—or extracting—resources above all else. Some call this system extractivism.

If extractivism has a father, it is probably an English thinker and scientist named Francis Bacon (1561–1626). He is credited with convincing the educated classes to give up old notions of the Earth as a life-giving mother who deserves our respect—and, at times, our fear. To Bacon, humans existed apart from the rest of the natural world, and the Earth existed to be used. Humans were her masters. He wrote in 1623 that if we studied nature, "we could lead and drive her."

The Earth, in this view, can be completely known. It can be controlled. This idea also appeared in the political writings of another Englishman, John Locke (1632–1704). Locke's thinking helped shape modern notions of liberty. Part of that liberty was "perfect freedom" to use the natural world in whatever way humans wanted. In France, meanwhile, the great philosopher René Descartes wrote that humans were nature's "masters and possessors."

Here's the trouble: if you are told that you own

something, or are "master" of it rather than are a part of it, you might think you can do whatever you want with it, without facing any consequences. Such thinking, especially Bacon's view of a knowable, controllable natural world, paved the way for the colonial activities of England and the other nations of Europe. Ships from these nations crisscrossed the globe to bring back the secrets of nature—and its wealth—to their crowns. At the same time, these voyages were also opportunities for the exploring countries to claim lands far from their own shores—as colonies. This turned the peoples already living on those lands into subjects of the colonizing nations, whether or not they wished to be.

Wealthy Europeans in this era imagined themselves to be all-powerful over nature and over non-Christian humans who lived in ways that were more connected to nature. That mood was captured by a clergyman who wrote in 1713, "We can, if need be, ransack the whole globe, penetrate into the bowels of the Earth, descend to the bottom of the deep, travel to the farthest regions of this world, to acquire wealth." It was a culture of triumphant taking, including seizing and enslaving non-European people. And with visions of Earth as a bottomless vending machine, full of resources waiting to be taken, the dream of extractivism was born.

All that was missing was a reliable source of energy to make that dream a reality.

REVOLUTION

For the first couple of decades, the new steam engine was a tough sell. Water wheels—the way most factories were powered—had a lot going for them. Water was free, while the steam engine needed to be fed with coal, which had to be constantly bought. The steam engine did not provide significantly more power either. Large water wheels, in fact, could produce several times more horsepower than their coal-powered rivals.

But as Britain's population grew, two things tipped the balance in favor of steam power. One advantage was that the new machine was not subject to nature's changes. As long as there was coal to feed it, the steam engine worked at the same rate all the time. The rate at which water flowed in rivers, or rose and fell with the seasons, did not matter.

The other advantage of the steam engine was that it worked anywhere. Water wheels had to be built alongside waterfalls or rapids, but steam-powered factories did not need any particular kind of geography. Factory owners could move their operations from remote towns or the countryside to big cities such as London. In the cities, with plenty of willing workers at hand, owners could easily fire troublemakers and crush workers' strikes. And fuel for the steam engines was no problem in cities, as well. After steam-powered locomotives were developed, new coal-burning trains hauled loads of coal from the mines to the new machinery of the industrial centers, wherever they were located.

In the same way, when Watt's engine was put in a boat, crews were free from depending on the winds. This made it even easier for Europeans to reach and claim countries in distant lands. At a meeting in honor of Watt in 1824, the Earl of Liverpool said, "Let the wind blow from whatever quarter it may, let the destination of our force be to whatever part of the world it may, you have the power and the means, by the Steam Engine, of applying that force at the proper time and in the proper manner."

It soon became clear, though, that, as you saw in chapter 3, fossil fuels required sacrifice zones—including the black lungs of the coal miners, the polluted waterways around the mines, and the enslaved bodies of Africans who were swept up in the Industrial Revolution, so you will soon see. But those prices were seen as worth paying for coal's promise of freedom and power for those who owned the mines, factories, and shipping companies. With their portable energy source, industry and colonialism could go wherever labor was cheapest and easiest to take advantage of, and wherever valuable resources could be had. Coal represented total control of other people and of nature. Bacon's dream had come true. It supercharged the Industrial Revolution.

At the same time, the sense that people could take whatever they needed from the natural world, whenever they wanted and for as long as they wanted, affected people at all levels of society. It went along with a desire to buy and possess new things, because coal-powered factories could now manufacture mass quantities of goods for people to consume.

No wonder that the time of Watt's steam engine was also a time of explosive growth in British manufacturing. Cotton is just one example. Britain imported raw cotton that was grown in other parts of the world. The vast majority of it was picked in the United States and the Caribbean by enslaved people who had been kidnapped in Africa, or who were descended from those Africans. Once the cotton reached Britain, textile mills turned it into finished cloth and manufactured clothing. British merchants then sold these products not just at home but around the world too.

This was a revolution. Two things made it possible:

coal at home to power the factories and the boats, and the labor of enslaved workers elsewhere to provide the cotton. Under this system, both the land and the people who worked it were treated as objects that could be exploited without limit.

This was the start of modern capitalism. The flood of new mass-produced manufactured products was matched by new markets to buy them. Before, most people had gotten what they needed from local craftspeople and small farms. Now the economy became centered on the market, the overall buying and selling of goods, sometimes items that had been shipped long distances.

One of the main features of this new economic model was—and still is—consumerism. In a market economy, people's role is to be consumers. Advertisements constantly urge them to buy new goods and replace old ones. Even some political speeches carry the message that it is citizens' duty to spend and buy.

The Industrial Revolution was not limited to Britain, home of Watt's steam engine. The revolution spread, first to western Europe and North America. And because it was powered by coal, this spreading revolution also marked the beginning of the human-made changes to the atmosphere that blankets our planet. That is because coal—like oil and natural gas, which came into wide use later—gives off greenhouse gases when it burns, and some of those gases remain in the air for a very long time.

Just how long a greenhouse gas remains in the air depends upon the type of gas. There are four main types: methane; nitrous oxide; carbon dioxide (CO_2); and a group of chemicals called fluorinated gases, which include hydrofluorocarbons, used in refrigeration and air-conditioning. Each type of greenhouse gas has a different staying power once it is part of the atmosphere.

Some methane comes from natural sources, such as the decay of plant material. But humans also produce methane by extracting fossil fuels from the ground, raising livestock, and piling up masses of waste in dumps and landfills. Methane lingers in the atmosphere for about twelve years.

Nitrous oxide lasts even longer, about 114 years. It is released into the air by nitrogen fertilizers, livestock waste, and some industrial processes.

Fluorinated gases play a smaller role in warming the world than the other greenhouse gases, but some of them linger in the air for thousands of years.

Worst is carbon dioxide (CO_2). Carbon dioxide is increased in the atmosphere by the use of fossil fuels and by deforestation, the large-scale cutting down of trees.

Some of this CO_2 is absorbed by the ocean, but the rest stays in the atmosphere for hundreds or even thousands of years.

This release of carbon dioxide is by far the biggest human-

Some of the sun's energy reflects back into space from the atmosphere. The rest reaches the Earth's surface, which reflects more of it back toward space. But greenhouse gases in the atmosphere trap part of this reflected energy, raising global temperatures. The major greenhouse gases are carbon dioxide, methane, nitrous oxide, and a group known by various names, including fluorinated gases and haloalkanes.

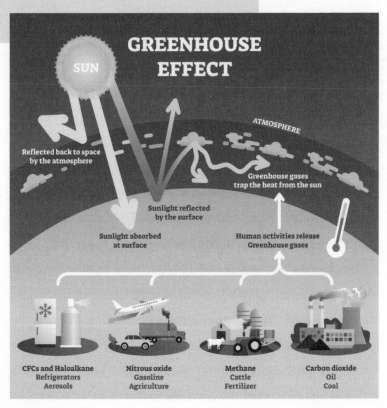

made contribution to climate change. And the most climate-changing activity of all is burning fossil fuels, especially coal. That brings the story back to coal, the steam engine, and what happened as the Industrial Revolution tightened its grip.

Deadly Pea-Soupers

Fog has been part of London's weather since ancient times. The British capital city sits in a valley with the River Thames flowing through it. When water vapor forms above the river, it can spread through the city, filling the streets with cool gray mist.

During the nineteenth century, though, London's fogs changed. They came more often, they were denser and thicker, and they sometimes had a biting sting that made people's eyes and throats burn. These were not fogs but smogs—combinations of fog mixed with smoke and soot, mostly from coal fires. The smogs' dirty yellowish color earned them the nickname "pea-soupers."

In her 2015 book *London Fog: The Biography,* Christine L. Corton writes that the peak years on average for London fogs and smogs were the 1890s. During that decade, the city was blanketed for an average of sixty-three days each year. But the worst year, by far, came later. It was 1952, the year of the Great Smog.

It started as a normal fog on December 5. Soon, though, the fog turned yellow-brown. It was mixing with pollution from the chimneys of houses, the smokestacks of factories, and the exhaust pipes of cars and buses. By the next day it was clear that this pea-souper was worse than usual. A weather system had stalled over the river valley, and there was no wind. A thirty-mile-wide (forty-eight-kilometer-wide) mass of cold, smoggy air was trapped over London as if in a bowl.

Like all pea-soupers, the Great Smog was a legacy of the Industrial Revolution, which had brought a steady increase in the use of coal by industry and power plants, as well as in the fireplaces and furnaces that people used to heat their homes. The coal that caused much of the pollution in nineteenth- and twentieth-century London was rich in sulfur, which gave the smog its yellowish color and its sting. Sulfur also added the stench of rotten eggs. The smog left a greasy black film on everything it touched, including people's faces.

Before long, the Great Smog was the worst that London had known. Drivers abandoned their cars because they could not see the streets. Trains and flights were canceled. Birds crashed into buildings and died. Movie theaters closed because the smog had gotten into buildings, blocking people's views of the screens. Crime did well, though. Criminals found it easy to disappear into the smog after a robbery or burglary.

Nelson's Column, a London landmark, was barely visible at noon during the Great Smog of 1952.

Finally, after five days, the weather changed, and wind swept the smog out of London. But the effects of the Great Smog would be felt for a long time. Thousands of people became sick and died from lung diseases such as bronchitis and pneumonia. Experts today think that the number of people who died because of the Great Smog was eight thousand or even higher. The very young, the elderly, and smokers were hardest hit.

Four years after the Great Smog, the British government passed a Clean Air Act to limit the use of coal in cities. And as coal faded from the scene, pea-soupers became less common. Additional deadly smogs and smog-related deaths occurred, but never another ordeal as severe as the Great Smog of 1952. After that major disaster had harmed thousands of people, the government stepped in—a sign that big change is possible when people's lives and health are at stake. And if that kind of change happened in London in the 1950s, it can happen anywhere today.

WARNING SIGNS

The Industrial Revolution was when Europeans first harnessed fossil-fuel power. For a couple of centuries after that, they seemed to have bent nature to their will, just as Francis Bacon had instructed. Since that time, though, we have remembered something that all of our ancestors used to know: all relationships in nature involve give-and-take. We now understand that the world is full of connections and that one thing always leads to another. When we harnessed fossil fuels, we did not do away with the give-and-take of relationships in nature. We merely delayed it.

For centuries we took fossil fuels out of the ground. Today the built-up effects of that burned carbon are giving us a more ferocious natural world: longer and drier droughts, fiercer wildfires, stronger storms, increased risk of poor health, and more. Esperanza Martínez, an ecologist from Ecuador, writes, "It has become clear over the last century that fossil fuels, the energy source of capitalism, destroy life—from the territories where they are extracted to the oceans and the atmosphere that absorb the waste."

But the signs of such effects appeared long ago. The earliest victims of coal were the miners who helped bring it out of the earth. Many died from a disease called black lung, which is as awful as it sounds. It is caused by exposure to coal dust, which damages lung tissue. Other early victims were the workers who toiled in the new factories and mills before there were laws in place to limit working hours, prevent child labor, or make workplaces safe. And of course the enslaved people who harvested the cotton, rubber, rice, and sugar cane that fed many of those factories were the greatest casualties of all. The environment, too, showed the scars of industrial progress. People grew used to seeing heaps of mining waste, soot-filled air, and polluted waterways instead of the natural scenery that had once surrounded them.

All of these things should have been early warnings that we were releasing poisons into the world, and the warning signs would increase in the twentieth century. However, most people didn't start to pay meaningful attention to what we were putting at risk until after the threat from climate change began to be understood. In the next chapter you'll see how scientists, writers, and people from many different age groups finally joined together in the late twentieth century to challenge the vending-machine view of nature—and to call for changes that would improve the health of both people and the planet.

CHAPTER 5

THE BATTLE TAKES SHAPE

Fossil fuels built the modern world. We all live inside the story written by coal, oil, and extractivism. Even in countries that do not have a lot of heavy industry, the air we breathe and the weather around us are affected by the global industrial economy. The phones, cars, and other goods we buy are products of that fossil-fuel-driven economy.

Within the story of fossil fuels and extractivism, people have fought for a more equal sharing of the profits. They have won some victories for the poor and the working classes, although most of these struggles did not confront the basic idea of extractivism itself. But by the 1980s, as concern about our dependence on fossil fuels grew, people began to challenge that very idea.

A fateful clash took shape. On one side were those who listened to the emerging warnings about fossil fuels and added new concerns about climate change. On the other side were those who ignored the warnings, shouted more loudly to drown the warnings out, or twisted the data to obscure the truth. This clash of values and ideas could not have come at a worse time in our history.

RISE OF A MOVEMENT

The movement often referred to as "environmentalism" is a network of many groups that want to protect the world and its resources from being devoured by human activity. Environmentalism's ideas are not new, but as a media phenomenon the movement came to maturity in the twentieth century. Did this new movement challenge the extractivists' view of nature as a bottomless source of resources and wealth? Not exactly.

Environmentalism's early history, especially in North America, had little to do with ordinary working-class people, much less the poor. It started out as a movement called conservationism in the late nineteenth and early twentieth centuries.

Conservationism was mostly made up of privileged, well-off men who enjoyed fishing, hunting, camping, and hiking. Although they realized that the rapid spread of industry threatened the wilderness they loved, most of them did not ask whether that spread across America's landscapes was a good thing, or whether it should be controlled. They just wanted to make sure that some spectacular places were set aside for them to enjoy. Their movement was not concerned with the fact that other places would be damaged by industry and development.

Noisy public protests were not how early conservationists achieved their goal. That would have been unseemly for a movement tied to the upper classes. No, they quietly persuaded other men like them to save a place they loved by turning it into a national or state park, or a private family nature park, or a game preserve. And often this meant that Indigenous People lost their right to hunt and fish on those grounds. There is a cruel irony to this because, as we have seen, Indigenous People living in what is now called North America were the continent's original environmentalists.

There were some early American ecological thinkers who argued for more than protecting isolated pieces of the landscape. Some of them were influenced by Asian beliefs that all life is interconnected, or by Native

American belief systems that see all living creatures as our relatives. In the middle of the nineteenth century, Henry David Thoreau of New England wrote, "The Earth I tread on is not a dead, inert mass. It is a body, has a spirit, is organic. . . ." This was the exact opposite of Francis Bacon's image of the Earth as an unliving machine whose mysteries could be mastered and plundered by the human mind.

Ideas similar to Thoreau's were held almost a century later by another American, Aldo Leopold, who was a key part of a second wave of environmentalism. His book *A Sand County Almanac* called for looking at the natural world in a way that "enlarges the boundaries of the community to include soils, waters, plants, and animals." This would change the role of humans from "conqueror of the land-community to plain member and citizen of it."

Leopold's writings had a huge influence on ecological thought, but, like Thoreau's earlier ideas, they did not slow down the galloping progress of industrialization. They were not tied to a large movement with support from much of the population. The dominant worldview continued to see humans as a conquering army, bringing the natural world under its control.

An important new challenge to this view appeared in 1962. That was when Rachel Carson, a scientist and writer, published *Silent Spring*. The book detailed the widespread use of chemicals such as DDT to kill insects. It showed the damage these insecticides did to bird life and more.

DDT being sprayed to control mosquitoes in Dhaka, the capital of Bangladesh. This toxic pesticide was banned in the US in 1972, ten years after Rachel Carson wrote about its devastating effects on wildlife in *Silent Spring*.

Carson's book boiled over with anger toward the chemical industry that used planes to spray from the air to wipe out insects, thoughtlessly endangering animal and human life in the process. Her focus was DDT, yet she knew that the problem was not one particular chemical. It was a way of thinking based on "control of nature." Her writing inspired a new generation of environmentalists to see themselves as part of a fragile planetary ecosystem, a web of interconnected life that we could not control without it collapsing.

Partly due to the wide influence of *Silent Spring*, around this time more people began questioning our treatment of the natural world and also the basic idea of extractivism—that there would always be more for us to take from nature. In North America, a new kind of environmental organization burst into life. Unlike the gentlemanly conservationists of the past, these activists did fight their battles in public and in the courts.

THE GOLDEN AGE OF ENVIRONMENTAL LAW

One of the new groups that came into being in the years after *Silent Spring* was the Environmental Defense Fund (EDF). A group of scrappy scientists and lawyers founded the organization in 1967. They heard Rachel Carson's warning and took action. The EDF filed the original lawsuit that led to the United States banning DDT as an insecticide. After the ban, many species of birds recovered. One of them was the bald eagle, the country's national bird.

When politicians of both parties were shown clear evidence of a serious problem that affected everyone, they asked themselves, "What can we do to stop it?" A wave of environmental victories followed.

The first environmental act to become federal law in the United States was the Federal Water Pollution Control Act of 1948. It was followed by the Clean Air Act of 1963. Then came the Wilderness Act of 1964, the Water Quality Act of 1965, the Air Quality Act of 1967, and the Wild and Scenic Rivers Act of 1968. These pieces of legislation were landmarks because they established the principle that the government had both the right and the responsibility to regulate how the entire country interacted with the environment. These victories seem almost impossible today, now that corporations and many more politicians are lined up against any kind of government regulation or control.

Environmental laws also reflect the fact that the environmental movement had diverse goals. Laws to limit the kinds and amounts of wastes and emissions that could go into air and water, for example, were largely aimed at protecting human health. The wilderness and rivers acts, in contrast, were aimed at preserving parts of the natural world. Twenty-three such diverse federal environmental acts were passed during the 1970s.

Then, in 1980, the Superfund Act required industry to make a small contribution toward cleaning up industrial areas that were dangerously full of toxic pollutants—the broad range of chemicals that can poison soil, water, air, and living things. The Superfund Act established the "polluter pays" principle that is central to climate justice.

These victories spilled over into Canada, which had its own flurry of environmental activism. And across the Atlantic Ocean, the European Community declared environmental protection a top priority in 1972. In the decades that followed, Europe became a leader in environmental law. The 1970s also brought landmarks in international environmental law, including an agreement to ban the commercial trade in endangered species, such as rare birds, or products made from endangered species, such as rhinoceros horn.

Environmental law did not take hold in many poorer parts of the world for another decade or so. In the meantime, communities defended the natural world directly. Women in Africa and India led creative campaigns against the loss of forests. Citizens of Brazil, Colombia, and Mexico organized large-scale resistance to nuclear power plants, dams, and other industrial developments. The process of developing stronger environmental laws in these countries followed.

This golden age of environmental law was based on two simple ideas. First, ban, or severely limit, the material or activity that creates the problem. Second, where possible, make the polluters pay for cleaning up their messes. Because large parts of the public supported these actions, the environmental movement won its greatest string of victories. But success brought major changes to the movement.

For many groups, the work of environmentalism changed. With the passage of laws that allowed polluters to be sued, environmentalists shifted their focus to legal actions rather than organizing protests and teach-ins. What had once been dismissed by some as a rabble of hippies became a movement of lawyers and lobbyists who spent their time meeting with politicians, jetting from one United Nations summit to the next, and striking deals with businesses. Many environmentalists prided themselves on being insiders who could wheel and deal with political leaders and the heads of corporations.

In the 1980s, this insider culture caused a shift. Some groups, including the EDF, took a new position toward business and corporations. In their view, the "new environmentalism" should not work to ban harmful activities. Instead, it would form partnerships with polluters.

Environmentalists could then persuade corporations to change their ways through voluntary measures. They would convince the polluters that they could save money and develop new products by going green—that is, by making their businesses more environmentally friendly.

This approach mirrored the pro-business thinking of the US government under Ronald Reagan, who was president from 1981 to 1989. It held that private solutions driven by the moneymaking motive and by the forces of the market are better than rules set out by the government.

The mainstream environmental movement had become Big Green. It now worked on different principles than the environmentalists of the 1960s and 1970s. The new principles were:

- Don't try to outlaw toxic or environmentally destructive things.

- Don't make enemies of business leaders and the politicians they support.

- Fight smaller battles. Maybe convince a polluter to do a few good things along with the bad things, or switch to a slightly less bad thing. Then you can call it a win for both sides.

Still, not every environmental group became business-friendly. Smaller, grassroots groups as well as a few of the large ones kept their focus on direct action against environmental harm. They continued to organize protests and file lawsuits. They encouraged consumers to boycott—or stop buying—products made by polluting companies.

Luckily, by this time the public in general was more familiar with environmentalism than it had been a generation earlier. Starting in 1970, the United States and many other nations had celebrated Earth Day every April as "a day for the environment." Schoolchildren grew up working on Earth Day projects—collecting litter from parks, for instance, or learning about wetlands. The words "environment" and "ecology" appeared in more and more conversations, classrooms, and news articles. Movements to "Save the Whales," or the pandas, or the rain forest seemed to pop up every week.

So when the words "global warming" and "climate change" showed up in conversations and news articles in the late 1980s, a lot of people were already used to thinking about environmental problems. But they had faced nothing on the scale of the looming climate crisis, when the environmental movement's drift toward business-oriented solutions would fall drastically short.

Young Environmentalists

for the Twenty-First Century

Aldo Leopold and Rachel Carson inspired environmentalists through the best-selling books they wrote. Some of today's young activists have already written books, but they also rely on marches, clubs, social media, and the internet to spread their messages and inspire people.

By the time he was seventeen, Jackson Hinkle of San Clemente, California, was taking action against plastic waste. He was a surfer, so he knew about the problem of plastic pollution in the ocean. As he learned more about water and the harms being done to it, he discovered that companies that sell bottled water are draining the local water sources of people around the world. He also learned that some plastic bottles can be a health risk as well as a waste problem.

Hinkle organized a march in his California county against the Dakota Access Pipeline, which threatened the water source of the Standing Rock

Sioux in North Dakota. (You will see more of the story of Standing Rock and the pipeline protests in the next chapter.) Hinkle also founded a club to campaign against plastic waste and to encourage people to use sustainable, reusable stainless steel water bottles.

Celeste Tinajero of Reno, Nevada, also joined an environmental club. She became part of Eco Warriors in high school after her older brother suggested it. The two of them then won first place in a competition sponsored by GREENevada. They used the $12,000 grant to make their high school more environmentally sustainable by updating its bathrooms, which wasted water with outdated sinks and toilets and also used wasteful paper towels. The following year they won second place in the same competition. This time they used the grant money to promote reusable water bottles for students. Tinajero went on to work for a local nonprofit group, designing education programs about living sustainably and cutting waste.

Writing a book about the natural world— together with the rest of her third-grade class—led Delaney Anne Reynolds of Miami, Florida, into environmental work at an early age. In middle school she helped build a solar power system for her school. Family trips to the ocean sparked her interest in the sea. She began researching marine biology, and this led her to an interest in the warming climate and its effects on the ocean—including rising seas.

Reynolds has since met with politicians, local business owners, and climate scientists to gain information and talk about solutions. By the age of seventeen she had written several other children's books about the environment. She had also delivered a TEDxYouth talk, which can be seen online, and had founded the Sink or Swim Project, which calls for education and political action to prevent Miami from sinking under the waters of climate change.

"I need your help," Reynolds says to other young people in her talk. "I need you to become involved, to speak up and out, because the time has come for our generation to solve this problem, to change old habits by getting rid of fossil fuels, to set politics aside, to invent new technologies. The time has come for our generation to decide whether we want our planet to sink, or swim."

These young climate activists, and many more like them, have shared their messages in a variety of ways, from marches and contest entries to books and websites. Their achievements show that what starts as a school project or a recreational hobby can turn into a crusade—or even a career—that can have as much impact as the activists that came before them.

IT WASN'T HUMAN NATURE

Time magazine did not name a Person of the Year in 1988. The honor went to the "Planet of the Year: Endangered Earth." The cover of the magazine showed a globe that was held together with string. In the background, the sun set in a blood-red sky.

"No single individual, no event, no movement captured imaginations or dominated headlines more than the clump of rock and soil and water and air that is our common home" was the explanation for *Time*'s choice.

Thirty years later, a journalist named Nathaniel Rich looked back on that moment in an article about the climate crisis for the *New York Times*. Back in 1988, the world seemed to truly understand that our pollution was dangerously overheating the planet. And governments were heading toward a tough, science-based global agreement to lower greenhouse gas emissions and head off the worst effects of climate change. The basic science of climate change had come to be understood and accepted during the 1980s.

The year 1988 was a watershed. That was when the director of NASA's Goddard Institute for Space Studies, James Hansen, spoke before the US Congress. Hansen said that he had "99 percent confidence" in "a real warming trend" that was linked to human activity. The statement was reported around the world. Now everyone knew that humans were causing the planet to get warmer.

Unlike today, political parties had not yet split into completely opposite camps. It really seemed as if the stage was set for politicians all over the world to come together and save what *Time* had called our "Endangered Earth." In fact, in 1988 hundreds of scientists and political advisers met in Toronto, Canada. At the historic World Conference on the Changing Atmosphere, they talked for the first time about targets for lowering emissions. Toward the end of 1988, the United Nations Intergovernmental Panel on Climate Change—the leading source of scientific information on the climate threat—held its first session.

When I look back at the climate news from 1988, it really did seem that a major change had been within reach. Now, though, I see that year as a turning point, because tragically, the chance for change slipped away. The United States abandoned international climate agreements that it had helped negotiate. The rest of the world settled for rules that had no real penalties if countries failed to live up to them. And predictably, they didn't.

What happened to the urgency and determination that so many people had felt about climate change at the end of the 1980s? In his 2018 article in the *New York Times*, Rich put forward a theory: "All the facts were known, and nothing stood in our way. Nothing, that is, except ourselves." Human beings, he wrote, "are incapable of sacrificing present convenience to forestall a penalty imposed on future generations."

In other words, people who are comfortable today aren't willing to change their way of life, even if it will harm everyone in the future. We are wired, Rich said, to "cast the long term out of our minds, as we might spit out a poison."

This is the "human nature" explanation of why governments have failed so spectacularly to take big, meaningful action against climate change. It says that we let our best chance to tackle climate change slip by because the harmful effects were in the future and did not seem as urgent as our need to continue our way of life. This explanation says that even when our survival may be at stake, we cannot cope with big, complicated problems that require all of us to work together.

But "human nature" is not to blame. Not everyone in 1988 threw their hands into the air and said, "Oh, well, there's nothing we can do." Political leaders in the developing world were calling for legally binding action. So were Indigenous Peoples.

Everything pointed toward real progress against climate change in 1988. So what went wrong? If human nature is not to blame, what is?

An epic case of historical bad timing.

Just as governments were getting serious about setting limits on fossil fuels, another global revolution went into overdrive, rearranging economies and societies. It grew out of the principles you read about in chapter 3—the ones that had contributed to weakening New Orleans's preparations for a hurricane. Governments and societies that adopt these principles are generally against regulations that limit or control what companies can do. They see the "free market"—the buying and selling of goods and services—as the solution to most problems. A related idea is that everyone in the world should adopt a way of life based on rapid consumption, such as fast food, fast fashion and electronics, and private cars rather than public transit and bicycles. Even though we know this way of life produces a lot of waste, it is thought to be good because it drives profit and economic growth.

These views eventually remade every major economy on the planet. They clashed with climate science, which told us that certain unregulated industries were heating the planet. They clashed with the idea that governments should then regulate those industries and companies for the public good. They also clashed with the idea that we all need to find less wasteful ways to live.

To meet the climate challenge, governments would have had to set stiff regulations on polluters so that the flow of greenhouse gases would be slowed. They would have had to invest in large-scale programs to help all of us change the way we power our lives, live in cities, and move ourselves around. But that would have meant a head-on battle with the economic ideas that had grown so strong. Meanwhile, countries signed trade agreements that made sensible climate actions—such as favoring local green industry, or refusing oil pipelines or other polluting projects—illegal under international law because they interfered with business.

Our planet was the victim of bad timing. At the very moment when James Hansen presented the world with clear evidence of climate change, corporations had grown so powerful that governments refused to do what was necessary to halt the warming.

And before long, scientists and activists had to fight

more than just business interests in the battle against climate change. They soon faced claims that the problem didn't even exist. This claim is called climate change denial. In spite of all the scientific evidence, some people deny that climate change is real.

DENIERS AND LIARS

When climate change began to make news, the corporate think tanks that had promoted the crusade for unregulated free markets saw the news as a threat to their ideas and projects. If "business as usual," based on burning fossil fuels, really was driving us toward climate tipping points that could threaten civilization, then that crusade would have to come to a screeching halt. The ideas behind the drive for unregulated free markets would lose their grip.

Our global economy would have to stop relying on fossil fuels. Pollution-creating activities would be widely banned, with big fines for violations. New government-funded programs would be created around the world to reshape industry, housing, and transportation. Funds would go toward green-energy projects such as wind farms and electric trains, for example, rather than toward benefits such as tax breaks for fossil-fuel companies. Properties and services that had once been run by governments but had been sold or leased to private industry, such as utility companies, railroads, and printing offices, might return to government control. And most threatening of all to a market-based economic system, we would all have to question the idea that endless consumption is good for us and can be sustained forever.

The very idea of climate change terrified some people. They called it a plot to "turn America socialist." (It isn't.) Some even claimed that those who warned of climate change secretly wanted to turn the country over to the United Nations. (They don't.)

Many corporate think tanks did not necessarily buy into these extreme ideas, but they did decide to champion the notion at the heart of them all: that climate change isn't real. Or, if global warming *is* real, they said, it's a natural process that has nothing to do with human activity. They promoted this message by unleashing a flood of books, articles, and free "teaching aids" for schools.

Some of these publications claimed that climate change is a hoax. Others tried to pick holes in the science of climate change. The evidence for global warming is wrong, they said. They sometimes focused on an example of scientists changing their projections when they gained new data, as if that meant that the whole idea of climate projections was wrong. They even simply pointed to a severe snowstorm and said, "See, global warming is a hoax," ignoring the fact that despite its name, global warming can make severe snowstorms *more* likely.

Some scientists have supported these views, but they are a very small minority. As of 2019, more than 97 percent of the world's climate scientists agree that climate change is real and that humans are either causing it or making it significantly worse.

Other pro-business publications about climate issues pretended to take the concerns seriously, but took a softer, friendlier approach to solving them. You may have come across this approach in videos or written materials directly aimed at schools and kids like you. Does this sound familiar—a vision of science and industry peacefully tackling environmental problems together? It would be great if that were true, but often such visions involve only surface-level changes.

Such nonsolutions are sometimes called greenwashing. An example would be a power company that spends $7 million to pass out booklets about energy-saving tips for families—but still gets 95 percent of its power from burning fossil fuels. That doesn't mean that the tips are useless, but it does mean that they're not enough to solve the biggest problems.

An energy company painted its oil-storage tank in Los Angeles to honor the twentieth anniversary of Earth Day in 1990—a classic example of greenwashing.

In the same way, kids are often taught about environmentalism not in terms of how whole industries and economic systems cause climate change but in terms of things individuals can do, such as recycling and riding a bike instead of driving a car. These actions are important, and we all need to do our part. But unless they are combined with bigger changes, they won't really rock business's boat—and therefore they won't make a significant impact on climate change. For this reason, it's a good idea always to check the sources of information. Are they believable? Do they have a track record of honesty? And, perhaps most important, does the source of the information have something to gain from what it is telling you?

WHO KNEW, AND WHEN DID THEY KNOW?

No matter what they said in public and in the propaganda they spread, behind closed doors the corporate bosses and scientists working at energy companies knew the truth. Links did exist between fossil fuels, greenhouse gas emissions, and climate change. We now know that the energy companies covered up the truth and spread misinformation. In 2015 a prize-winning news organization called InsideClimate News published reports about what the energy industry knew, and when.

InsideClimate News showed that the Exxon Corporation knew about the link between fossil fuels and climate change decades ago. (Today the corporation is called ExxonMobil. It is the world's largest oil and gas company.) An Exxon scientist told the company's executives in 1977, "There is general scientific agreement that the most likely manner in which mankind is influencing the global climate is through carbon dioxide release from the burning of fossil fuels." In other words, Exxon's own product was warming the planet.

A year later the same scientist wrote a more detailed report for Exxon's scientists and managers. It warned that changes in energy planning and use would soon become necessary.

At first the corporation did not deny climate change. Instead, Exxon launched a serious research program to better understand it. Company scientists studied the effects of carbon dioxide emissions on the atmosphere and the planet. Exxon even fitted an oil tanker with scientific equipment to look into the question of whether the oceans were getting warmer because of increased greenhouse gases.

Exxon scientists also helped develop new software programs to model climate change. Some of the research that the company did or paid for was even published in scientific journals in the early 1980s.

But two things changed Exxon's approach to the issue. First, oil prices worldwide dropped in the mid-1980s, and the company's profits went down. It laid off many employees, including some climate researchers. Second, in 1988, NASA scientist James Hansen warned the US Congress about fossil fuels and climate change. During that hearing, Senator Tim Wirth of Colorado said, "Congress must begin to consider how we are going to slow or halt that warming trend." This alarmed the energy industry. The comment suggested that the government might enact new regulations that could affect business more than whatever the companies might voluntarily do.

Suddenly Exxon, like all the other big energy companies, started to say that the science of climate change was not clear or certain. They argued that it would be foolish to take drastic action without "more information." In 1997 the chief executive of Exxon said, "We need to understand the issue better, and fortunately, we have time. It is highly unlikely that the temperature in the middle of the next century will be significantly affected whether policies are enacted now or 20 years from now."

But the energy companies knew this was not true. A science team from Mobil had written a report in 1995 that was shared with the other energy companies. It said, "The scientific basis for the Greenhouse Effect and the potential impact of human emissions of greenhouse gases such as CO_2 on climate is well established and cannot be denied."

Still, the energy companies launched a major effort to create a fog of climate doubt, if not outright climate denial. Their goal was to keep governments from setting stricter limits on greenhouse gas emissions or making new rules about the extraction of oil, natural gas, and coal in the future. At the same time, these companies worked to give their public images a green shine. From

1989 to 2019, the five biggest oil companies in the world spent $3.6 billion on advertising that boasted about their efforts to help the environment. Exxon, for example, talked about how it was buying solar power and wind power in Texas. What it didn't say was that it used that power to drill for more oil. In spite of their greenwashing, the oil companies continued to place profits over people and the planet.

Can anything be done to rein in the powerful fossil-fuel industry? One answer may be seen in what happened to the powerful tobacco industry in the 1990s. By that time, the scientific evidence about tobacco was clear: it is seriously harmful to human health. But evidence showed that the industry had known about tobacco's harmful effects, such as lung cancer, for a long time. The tobacco companies had covered up that knowledge because they'd wanted people to keep smoking or start smoking so that the companies could continue to profit.

So Congress investigated the tobacco industry. The congressional investigation led to tighter regulation of tobacco sales. It also led to lawsuits against the tobacco companies and huge payouts by those companies.

Will what happened to Big Tobacco also happen to Big Oil? After investigative journalists uncovered documents about the oil and gas industry's suppression of its climate change knowledge, Congress took a step toward investigating the industry in October 2019. A committee held a hearing on Examining the Oil Industry's Efforts to Suppress the Truth about Climate Change. One committee member, Representative Alexandria Ocasio-Cortez, questioned a climate scientist who had worked with Exxon in the 1980s. She asked about an Exxon memo from 1982 that had come to light. It contained a prediction that global temperatures would increase by 1°C by the year 2019—which they had. "We were excellent scientists," the scientist said. He knew their prediction had come to pass.

The congressional investigation is still going on, but one thing is clear: Exxon knew. And it was not alone. Shell is a major international energy company headquartered in the Netherlands. In 2020 the head of the Shell corporation told a reporter, "Yeah, we knew. Everybody knew. And somehow we all ignored it."

As activists rallied under the banner #ExxonKnew, the State of New York sued Exxon, claiming the company had given its investors false or misleading information about the costs and risks of climate change. In late 2019 that case ended in a victory for Exxon, but the energy industry's legal battles were just beginning.

These young "Exxon Knew" marchers in 2015 also knew—that Exxon had covered up the truth about fossil fuels and climate change.

Exxon, BP, Chevron, and other companies are facing dozens of lawsuits. Some of these lawsuits accuse the companies of deceiving the public. Others accuse them of contributing to the losses that cities and states have suffered because of climate change. Some lawsuits ask the companies to pay part of the cost of adjusting to climate change, such as building seawalls in coastal communities threatened by rising tides.

People in other countries are bringing legal challenges

to the industry too. In the Netherlands, for example, seventeen thousand citizens have filed a lawsuit against Shell.

The question of how much harm the energy companies did by concealing information, and what price they ought to pay for it, will be argued in courts around the world for years.

Activists against Big Oil

While lawsuits against the major energy companies work their way through court systems, protesters are not waiting. They are taking direct action to call the public's attention to Big Oil's role in the climate crisis.

In September 2019, Greenpeace activists hung streaming cloth banners and their own bodies (in safety harnesses) from a bridge over a channel in Houston, Texas. The red, orange, and yellow banners represented "the sun setting on the age of oil," said Greenpeace.

The channel is part of a major shipping route for oil tankers. About 12 percent of the oil that is refined in the United States passes through this channel. The activists' blockade partially closed the channel and prevented ships from passing through for eighteen hours. They had made a statement.

But Texas had passed a new law that made it illegal to protest near pipelines or any other feature considered important to the gas and oil industry. More than a dozen people were arrested. A number of other states have passed similar laws to keep protesters quiet. Lawmakers often claim that these laws are meant to keep protesters safe by keeping them away from possible hazards such as fuel leaks. Activists say that the laws show that business interests carry more weight with some governments than individual rights and the health of the planet.

But young activists are undaunted. At a football game between two of the most elite universities in the United States, hundreds of students and former students from Harvard and Yale left the stands to protest their schools' investments in fossil fuels. They rushed onto the field and delayed the game for an hour, chanting, "Hey hey! Ho ho! Fossil fuels have got to go!"

A few months after that, students from Harvard Law School demonstrated at an event put on by a law firm that has represented Exxon. With a banner that read "#DropExxon," the protesters encouraged young lawyers to follow their example and refuse to work for any company that has taken money from corporate polluters. Like many other activists today, they live-streamed their protest on the internet to make sure their voices were heard.

Then in Scotland in early January 2020, the environmental and climate group Extinction Rebellion carried out a series of "actions focusing on the fossil fuel industry and its driving role in the climate crisis." Protesters, including many young people, blocked the entrance to Shell's headquarters in Aberdeen in what police called a peaceful protest. Other protesters climbed aboard an oil-drilling rig that was moored in the harbor at Dundee. The rig was scheduled to be towed out to sea for use by Shell. Seven people later appeared in court to face charges for occupying the rig.

Although the Extinction Rebellion activists didn't stop the rig from being moved, they did get the chance to tell newspapers and television reporters why they felt it was important to stop drilling for oil around Scotland.

While big demonstrations or stunts do draw attention, they aren't the only way to get the message across. A majority of young activists focus on other equally determined acts, such as writing letters to lawmakers and political candidates, marching in school strikes, and researching and sharing climate information with their peers and families. These actions also raise awareness about climate change and inspire people to take action. A 2019 study found that when parents are skeptical about the seriousness of climate change, some of the people most likely to change their minds are their own children. Activism does not have to be dramatic to be meaningful.

A NEW RISING

Think again of that turning-point year of 1988, when the US Congress heard a statement about human-caused climate change. Imagine that the nations of the world had come together then and taken real action to lower greenhouse gas emissions.

The climate crisis today would be less severe. We would be much further along in the work of preventing catastrophe. Now imagine that those steps had been taken even earlier, in 1977, when a scientist at Exxon had first talked to his bosses about the problem of fossil fuels and greenhouse gases.

Because of the powerful influence of pro-business ideas, we lost whole decades that could have been spent lowering emissions. We could have made the worst future effects of climate change far less likely.

We can't change that now. That's the bad news—and you have a right to be angry about it.

The good news is that there is still a great deal we can do about climate change today.

The problem in 1988 wasn't "human nature," something that we can't change. As we have seen, the problem was companies and governmental policies that valued markets and profits over people and the planet. And that *is* something we can question, challenge, and change.

A young and growing movement is rising in the United States and many other countries. Young people are doing more than saying no to the polluters and politicians of the present. They are not accepting greenwashing or propaganda or denials. Instead, they are mapping out and fighting for a better future. And while earlier generations of activists focused on the symptoms of environmental and climate problems, your generation is taking aim at the very system that values profits over lives and our climate future.

The message of the school strikes and other youth movements is that a great many young people are ready for that kind of deep change. They are calling for a new politics and a new economics with new values, with decisions based on justice and on the world's carbon budget. "But that is not enough," says Greta Thunberg. "We need a whole new way of thinking. . . . We must stop competing with each other. We need to start cooperating and sharing the remaining resources."

Today is different from 1988, and not just because we are decades further into the climate crisis. It's different because of your generation's fierce insistence on deep change. The youth climate movement and other youth-led movements fighting racial and gender violence and discrimination are mighty forces pushing us all toward a better future.

CHAPTER 6

PROTECTING THEIR HOMES—AND THE PLANET

A scientist with pink hair and a serious expression had come to San Francisco to give a talk.

His name was Brad Werner. He was a researcher at the University of California at San Diego. It was December 2012, and twenty-four thousand scientists had gathered for a meeting. The schedule was packed with talks, but Werner's had drawn a lot of attention because of its topic. He was going to talk about the fate of the planet.

Standing at the front of the conference room, Werner took the crowd through the advanced computer model he was using to predict this. A lot of the details would be mystifying to those who are new to Werner's subject of research, which is complex systems theory. (Systems theory is the study of complicated systems with many parts that interact with each other. One example of a complex system is weather, which is the interplay of parts such as temperature, air currents, ocean currents, geography, and more.)

The bottom line of Werner's presentation, though, was clear. A global economy based on fossil-fuel energy, free-market economics, and consumerism has made it easy to use up the Earth's resources—so easy that the balance between Earth's resources and ecosystems on one hand and human consumption on the other is becoming unstable.

But one piece of Werner's complex model offered hope. He called it "resistance." By this he meant movements of people or groups whose actions do not fit within the mainstream economic culture. Those actions could include environmental protests, blockades, and mass uprisings by Indigenous Peoples, workers, and others. The most likely way to slow down an economic machine that is careening out of control is a resistance movement. It would add "friction," as Werner said—grit in the gears of the machine.

Werner pointed out that past social movements

have changed the direction of mainstream culture. The abolitionist movement ended slavery. The civil rights movement won equality under the law for Black Americans. By proving to national leaders that many people not only supported but demanded change, these movements led to the passage of new laws that made the change happen. Werner said, "If we're thinking about the future of the Earth, and the future of our coupling to the environment, we have to include resistance as part of that dynamics."

In other words, only social movements can turn the tide of climate change now.

With the climate crisis becoming ever more urgent, those movements are gathering speed. Young people are not simply joining them. Often they are leading the way.

This chapter takes a close look at several recent acts of resistance to climate change and injustice. Each of these acts involved young people who wanted to protect their homes—and help save the planet while doing so. Each of them was a piece of grit in the gears, a challenge to the economic ideas and the fossil-fuel-based industries that have contributed so much to our current crisis. These activists stood up, spoke out, and tested the power of resistance. They mapped out some of the paths that can lead us to a better climate future.

THE HEILTSUK NATION: THE RIGHT TO SAY NO

Bella Bella, also known as Waglisla, is a state-sanctioned reserve for the Heiltsuk Nation, one of the many Nations located on the coast of British Columbia. It is a remote island community, a place of deep fjords and lush evergreen forests reaching to the sea. In 2012 it had 1,905 residents. On an April day, about a third of them were out in Bella Bella's streets. That was the day a three-person

The remote Canadian island town of Bella Bella draws life from the waters around it. When those waters were threatened, the community fought for them.

review panel flew into town to hold a hearing about an oil pipeline.

The pipeline was being planned by Enbridge, a Canadian company that builds pipelines and storage centers for oil. The planned pipeline was called the Northern Gateway. It would run through the western part of Canada for 731 miles (1,176 kilometers) from Edmonton, in the neighboring province of Alberta, to the coast of British Columbia. On the coast, oil extracted from tar sands in Alberta would be gathered and loaded onto ocean-going tankers and shipped around the world. The pipeline would carry 525,000 barrels of oil a day.

The review panel that had just arrived would tell the Canadian government whether the plan should go ahead or not. For months the panel had been holding hearings along the route that the pipeline and tankers would follow. Now its members had reached the end of the line.

Bella Bella is 124 miles (200 kilometers) south of the point where the Northern Gateway would meet the sea. But the Pacific waters that are the town's front yard were in the path that those tankers would take. Those waters are sprinkled with islands and rocky reefs. The waters swirl with changing currents. And the tankers would be huge. They could carry 75 percent more crude oil than the *Exxon Valdez*, a tanker that caused a widespread and long-lasting environmental disaster when it spilled oil in Alaskan waters in 1989.

The Heiltsuk Peoples living in Bella Bella had deep concerns about the potential for a spill in their waters. And they were ready to share those concerns with the review board.

A line of Heiltsuk chiefs, wearing traditional embroidered robes and headdresses and hats of woven cedar, welcomed the review board at the airport with a dance. Drummers and singers backed them up. A large crowd of demonstrators waited behind a chain-link fence, holding canoe paddles and anti-pipeline signs.

Behind the chiefs stood a twenty-five-year-old woman named Jess Housty. She had helped energize the community to meet with the review panel. For Housty, the scene at the airport was the result of "a huge planning effort driven by our whole community." But young people had taken the lead, turning their school into a hub of organizing. They'd researched the history of oil spills from pipelines and tankers. They'd painted signs. They'd written essays about how an oil spill in their waters would damage not only the ecosystem but also their way of life. Both the ancient culture of the Heiltsuk Peoples and their modern livelihoods are tied to the ecosystem, especially to its herring and sockeye salmon.

Teachers said that no issue had ever engaged the community's young people as much as the pipeline proposal.

"As a community," Housty later said, "we were prepared to stand up with dignity and integrity to be witnesses for the lands and waters that sustained our ancestors—that sustain us—that we believe should sustain our future generations."

Indigenous activists were a major part of efforts to block Canada's Northern Gateway pipeline, as in this 2012 protest in Victoria, British Columbia.

The high level of community involvement made what happened next all the more crushing. The review panel refused the invitation to the feast that had been planned for the evening. It also canceled the pipeline hearing for which the community had been preparing for months.

Why?

The visitors said they felt unsafe after their five-minute drive from the airport into town. They had passed hundreds of people, including children, holding signs: OIL IS DEATH, WE HAVE A MORAL RIGHT TO SAY NO, KEEP OUR OCEANS BLUE, and I CAN'T DRINK OIL. One protester thought the panel members weren't bothering to look out the window, so he slapped the side of their van as it drove by. Did the panel members mistake his slap for a gunshot, as some people later said? Police who had been there, though, said that the protest was not violent. There had been no threat to anyone's safety.

Many of the Heiltsuk citizens were shocked by the way the spirit of their protest had been misunderstood. They felt that when the panel members had looked out the van windows, they'd seen nothing but a mob of "angry Indians" who wanted to vent hatred at anyone linked to the pipeline. Their demonstration, though, had been mainly about love—their love for their home, and its entire web of life, in a breathtakingly beautiful part of the world.

In the end, the hearing was held after all, but the community had lost a day and a half of its scheduled time. Many people had no chance to be heard in person.

Still, Jess Housty—who was elected to the Heiltsuk Tribal Council as its youngest member—traveled for a full day to another town to speak before the review panel. Her message was clear:

> *When my children are born, I want them to be born into a world where hope and transformation are possible. I want them to be born into a world where stories still have power. I want them to grow up able to be Heiltsuk in every sense of the word. To practice the customs and understand the identity that has made our people strong for hundreds of generations.*
>
> *This cannot happen if we do not sustain the integrity of our territory, the lands and waters, and the stewardship practices that link our people to the landscape. On behalf of the young people in my community, I respectfully disagree with the notion that there is any compensation to be made for the loss of our identity, for the loss of our right to be Heiltsuk.*

More than a thousand people spoke to the review panel at its hearings in British Columbia. Only two of them supported the pipeline. One poll showed that eight out of ten people in British Columbia did not want more oil tankers along their coastline.

So what did the review panel recommend to Canada's federal government? That the pipeline should go ahead. Many Canadians saw this as a clear sign that the decision was about money and power, not about the environment or the will of the people.

The government approved the pipeline in 2014. However, Enbridge, the company that wanted to build the Northern Gateway, would have to meet 209 conditions, such as creating plans for safeguarding caribou habitat and consulting with members of the Heiltsuk Nation and other Indigenous Peoples who would be affected by the pipeline.

A bigger obstacle for the company, though, was that a large part of the public did not stop protesting the pipeline. Indigenous Peoples from many groups united against Northern Gateway, still fearing that spills would damage land, wildlife, and the Fraser River, as well as coastal waters. Their concerns were reasonable. The Canada Energy Regulator, the government agency responsible for monitoring the pipelines that carry oil or liquefied natural gas in Canada, recorded between 54 and 175 leaks, spills, or fires each year from 2008 to 2019.

Environmental organizations, Indigenous Peoples, and groups of citizens took their protest to court and sued to stop the building of the pipeline. The cases went to trial in British Columbia and in the federal justice system of Canada. In 2016 the Federal Court of Appeal overturned the government's approval of the pipeline.

The fight of the Standing Rock Sioux of North Dakota to protect their water drew supporters from around the world, including Indigenous protesters in Toronto, Canada.

It said that Enbridge had not properly consulted with Indigenous Peoples over the project.

Finally, after this victory, the company stopped fighting for the pipeline. In 2019 it said that it had no plans to reopen the Northern Gateway project. Instead, it would focus on smaller pipelines.

Every pipeline is a risk, as Enbridge knows. In 2010 a massive spill from one of its pipelines contaminated forty miles (sixty-four kilometers) of the Kalamazoo River in Michigan with heavy oil from the tar sands. Cleanup took years and cost more than a billion dollars. Enbridge settled claims against it for $177 million, including fines.

But for the Heiltsuk Nation, at least, the threat of a new pipeline is in the past. People there won a victory when they claimed their right to say no.

STANDING ROCK: THE WATER PROTECTORS

Like the story of the Northern Gateway, the story of Standing Rock is about a pipeline and a protest.

Although the protest eventually grew to include environmentalists, military veterans, celebrities, and people from around the world, it began with Indigenous People. At its heart was a desperate attempt by the Standing Rock Sioux of North Dakota to protect their land—and especially their water.

A Texas company called Energy Transfer wanted to build the Dakota Access Pipeline (DAPL) to connect oil fields in North Dakota to an oil storage center in Illinois. The 1,172-mile (1,886-kilometer) pipeline would be buried in the ground. It would be drilled beneath hundreds of lakes or waterways, including the Missouri, Mississippi, and Illinois Rivers. At thirty inches (seventy-six centimeters) wide, the DAPL could move up to 570,000 barrels of oil each day.

The risks of pipelines are well known. Leaks caused by rust or other damage spill oil or liquefied natural gas into soil or water, where they are dangerous or toxic to humans and wildlife. Such contamination can linger for years. And because these substances are flammable, fires can occur at the site of a leak or fault in the pipeline. The US Department of Transportation's Pipeline and Hazardous Materials Safety Administration, which monitors pipelines in the United States, recorded 12,312 incidents from 2000 to 2019. These incidents led to 308 deaths, 1,222 injuries, and $9.5 billion in damages.

In spite of these risks, Energy Transfer claimed that the Dakota Access Pipeline would be safe. They said building it would create thousands of short-term jobs and up to fifty permanent jobs in North and South Dakota, Iowa, and Illinois, the states along the pipeline's path.

At first, the pipeline was going to pass near Bismarck, North Dakota, but the US Army Corps of Engineers turned down that plan because it feared that leaks from the pipeline could contaminate the city's water supply. A new plan would run the pipeline along the northern tip of the Standing Rock Sioux Reservation, which straddles the border between the two Dakotas.

Instead of threatening a city with a majority white population, now the DAPL would threaten Lake Oahe, the only source of drinking water for the Standing Rock Sioux. Their sacred and cultural sites would also be at risk. This was environmental racism, out in the open.

People protested the pipeline at many points along its route, but the long and determined protest at Standing Rock captured the attention of the world. While teams of lawyers and environmentalists tried to block or delay the pipeline on legal grounds, in April 2016 young people of Standing Rock started the #NoDAPL protest campaign against the pipeline. They called for the world to join them in blocking construction of the pipeline.

LaDonna Brave Bull Allard, the tribe's official historian, opened the first camp for this resistance movement on her land. It was called Sacred Stone Camp. The movement's slogan, in the Lakota language, was

Mni wiconi—"Water Is Life." The protesters described themselves as water protectors.

People gathered at Sacred Stone and in satellite camps to organize their protests but also to work, teach, and learn. For Indigenous youth, the gatherings were a way to connect more deeply with their own culture, to live on the land, to follow traditions and ceremonies. For non-Indigenous people, it was a chance to learn skills and knowledge they didn't have.

Brave Bull Allard watched as her grandchildren taught non-Indigenous people how to chop wood. She taught hundreds of visitors what she considered basic survival skills, such as how to use sage as a natural disinfectant and how to stay warm and dry in North Dakota's vicious storms. Everyone, she instructed, needed "at least six tarps."

When I arrived at Standing Rock, Brave Bull Allard told me she had come to understand that, although stopping the pipeline was crucial, something greater was happening in the camps. People were learning to live in community with the land. Practical skills, such as cooking and serving meals to thousands of people, were inspiring, but participants were also being exposed to the traditions and ceremonies that her people had protected, despite hundreds of years of attacks on Indigenous People and cultures. Being in the camps meant bonding together in a shared purpose, and teaching and learning in new ways. From seminars on nonviolence to drumming around a sacred fire, much of this knowledge was shared with the world on the visitors' social media feeds.

Resistance to the pipeline continued, even when security forces hired by the pipeline company set attack dogs loose on the water protectors. But in the fall of 2016 things got worse as soldiers and riot police forcibly cleared a camp that sat directly on the pipeline's path. The assault on the protest did not end there. A month later, in freezing weather, police drenched protectors with water cannons. At the time it was the most violent use of state power against demonstrators in recent US history.

North Dakota's governor then doubled down and issued orders to clear the camps entirely in early December. The movement was to be crushed, with force.

I and many other people went to North Dakota to stand with the water protectors. A convoy of about two thousand military veterans also joined the resistance. They said they had sworn to serve and protect the Constitution. After seeing video of peaceful Indigenous water protectors being brutally attacked, fired on with rubber bullets and pepper spray, and blasted with water cannons, these veterans had decided their duty now was to stand up to the very government that had sent them to war.

Despite being drenched by blasts from law enforcement's water cannons, Standing Rock protesters held the line in freezing temperatures.

By the time I arrived, the network of camps had grown to about ten thousand people. Participants lived in tents, tepees, and yurts. The main camp was a hive of orderly activity. Volunteer cooks served meals. Groups gathered for political study. Drummers gathered around a sacred fire, tending to the flames so that they would never go out. Despite the threats, the protesters were not going anywhere.

On December 5, after months of resistance, the water protectors learned that the administration of President

Barack Obama had refused to give Energy Transfer a permit that the company needed to drive the pipeline under the Missouri River at Lake Oahe—one of the last stretches yet to be built.

I will never forget the experience of being at the main camp when the news arrived. I happened to be standing with Tokata Iron Eyes, a thirteen-year-old from Standing Rock who had helped start the movement against the pipeline. I turned on my phone video and asked her how she felt about the breaking news. "Like I have my future back," she said, and then she burst into tears. I did too.

The battle seemed to be won—but was it?

Obama would be president for just a few more weeks. Republican Donald Trump had already been elected as the next president. He was known to be a friend of the oil and gas industry, and the top executive of Energy Transfer had made a large donation to his campaign. Some protesters feared that their victory would be snatched away, so they remained in the camp.

They were right.

In January 2017, Trump reversed Obama's decision. The pipeline would go ahead. At the end of February, soldiers and law enforcement removed the protesters who remained. The DAPL was completed. It went into operation in June. A report in early 2018 said that it had leaked at least five times during 2017.

The pipeline was built, but the Standing Rock Sioux continued to challenge it in the courts. In June 2020 a federal judge ruled that in permitting the pipeline, the US Army Corps of Engineers had violated the National Environmental Policy Act and had not properly reported the potential hazards of the project. The judge ordered the pipeline shut down until a full environmental analysis was complete—a process that could take several years. The ruling was a hard-fought victory for the Standing Rock Sioux and for all those who had joined the #NoDAPL campaign.

At the same time, pressure from the public had caused investors to divest—to pull about $80 million out of banks that had loaned money to the DAPL project. Protesters who urge banks and other lenders to divest from fossil-fuel projects do not always succeed in stopping those projects, but they discourage lenders from supporting future projects. Meanwhile, the Standing Rock Sioux have several projects underway to power their community with clean solar energy rather than use the fossil fuels that have threatened their water.

During those months at Standing Rock, the water protectors created a model of resistance that said both no and yes. No to a threat in the moment, but yes to building a world that we want and need.

"We are here to protect the Earth and the water," LaDonna Brave Bull Allard said. "This is why we are still alive. To do this very thing we are doing. To help humanity answer its most pressing question: how do we live with the Earth again, not against it?"

A Long Run for the Future

When Alice Brown Otter stood in the spotlight at the Oscars ceremony in Hollywood, she was fourteen years old. Almost two years earlier, in August 2016, she had run 1,519 miles (2,445 km) from North Dakota to Washington, DC.

Brown Otter was one of about thirty young Indigenous People who had run to the nation's capital with a petition signed by 140,000 people. It asked the Army Corps of Engineers to stop work on the Dakota Access Pipeline because a leak or spill from the pipeline near the Standing Rock Sioux Reservation could contaminate the reservation's only water source.

That long run was not the beginning of Brown Otter's activism, and it wasn't the end. She explained, "It's normal for a human to stand up for the Earth that they live on. It's actually a gift to be here. It's just giving back." She believes young people should have more of a voice in decision making. "We're gonna be the next adults."

In early 2018, a year after President Trump had allowed the pipeline to be completed, Brown Otter was one of ten activists invited to the annual Oscars ceremony in Hollywood. They took the stage with performers Common and Andra Day, who sang the song "Stand Up for Something" from the movie *Marshall*, the story of civil rights leader and Supreme Court Justice Thurgood Marshall.

"It was really nerve-wracking at first," said Brown Otter, "but just having a lot of people up on stage with you fighting for different causes but who want the same thing: a different change in the world. It was just such an amazing experience." Her experience shows that making a difference sometimes means simply putting one foot in front of the other, again and again—and shows that you may be surprised at where your path of protest takes you.

THE *JULIANA* CASE: KIDS TAKE IT TO COURT

Can kids sue the United States government for failing to act against climate change? Twenty-one young people asked that question when they launched the climate lawsuit *Juliana v. United States* in 2015.

Young people from ten states filed the suit against the government in the US District Court in Oregon, home of eleven of the plaintiffs—the people filing the lawsuit. The case takes its name from one of them, Kelsey Juliana. Their legal services were provided by a law group that supports conservation, climate justice, and the right of young people to have a voice in the issues that will shape their futures.

The lawsuit claimed that the government had known for decades that carbon dioxide pollution from fossil fuels was causing "catastrophic climate change." Yet the government continued to make climate change worse. It aided and encouraged more fossil-fuel extraction, including on lands owned by the public and managed by government agencies.

The government's actions were a violation of rights guaranteed by the US Constitution, said the lawsuit. Those actions interfered with the young people's "fundamental right of citizens to be free from government actions that harm life, liberty, and property." They also argued that the government had violated its duty as a steward of public lands.

The lawsuit listed the damages and losses each of the young people was experiencing because of climate change. It gave evidence for human-caused climate change and for the government's knowledge of that evidence. One of the plaintiffs is the granddaughter of James Hansen, the famous climate scientist you read about in chapter 5. He testified in the case.

What did the kids want? They asked the court to do three main things. First, order the government to stop violating the Constitution. Second, declare that plans for a fossil-fuel development called Jordan Cove on the Oregon coast were unconstitutional and must stop. Third, order the government to prepare a plan for lowering fossil-fuel emissions.

The lawsuit was filed in August 2015. Then came a long, complicated series of legal moves and countermoves. Along the way, the administrations of two presidents, Barack Obama and Donald Trump, tried repeatedly to get the case thrown out of court.

They did not succeed. After several delays, the trial was finally set to take place in October 2018. The Trump administration applied to the United States Supreme Court to halt the case or postpone it again, but the court ruled that the case would proceed. (It would take place in a lower federal court, as planned, and not before the Supreme Court.) Vic Barrett from New York, one of the twenty-one young people who had filed the lawsuit, said,

"The constitutional rights of my fellow plaintiffs and I are at stake in this case, and I am glad that the Supreme Court of the United States agrees that those rights should be evaluated at trial. This lawsuit becomes more urgent every day as climate change increasingly harms us."

The government did not stop. Once again, the case was delayed. This time, lawyers for the Trump administration shifted their request for a halt or delay to a lower court, the Ninth Circuit Court of Appeals. This court issued an order called a "stay." The trial was put on hold while three judges of the Ninth Circuit heard arguments about whether or not the lawsuit should go ahead.

Legal back-and-forth ate up all of 2019. But the youth-led climate group Zero Hour lost no time. It started a campaign asking thousands of young people from across the country to add their names to a "friend of the court" document in support of the *Juliana* youths. Other organizations and activist communities did the same. The court received fifteen such documents.

In January 2020 the three-judge panel of the Ninth Circuit Court of Appeals gave its ruling on whether the case could go ahead. The panel agreed with the young *Juliana* plaintiffs that climate change is real. However, two of the three judges ruled that it was beyond the power of a federal court to give them the remedies they sought for the losses and harms they have suffered from climate change. Their written opinion said, "The panel reluctantly concluded that the plaintiffs' case must be made to the political branches or to the electorate at large."

In other words, these two judges told the kids to take it to Congress, the president, or the voters.

The third judge did not agree. She wrote in her dissenting opinion, "It is as if an asteroid were barreling toward Earth and the government decided to shut down our only defenses. Seeking to quash this suit, the government bluntly insists that it has the absolute and unreviewable power to destroy the nation." But her view was in the minority, and the case was dismissed.

By that time, Kelsey Juliana was twenty-three. She and the other plaintiffs had spent more than four years pushing the *Juliana* case forward. She said, "I am disappointed that these judges would find that federal courts can't protect America's youth, even when a constitutional right has been violated." But even though it had taken a long time to get this no, the young people and their lawyers did not give up.

"The *Juliana* case is far from over," said one of the lead attorneys. "The Youth Plaintiffs will be asking the full court of the Ninth Circuit to review this decision and its catastrophic implications for our constitutional democracy."

The young people of the *Juliana* case have learned that seeking justice in the courts can be a long and winding path, but it is one they and their legal team plan to follow to the very end.

Many legal experts think that more climate lawsuits are likely, especially if the president and Congress continue to do nothing about climate change. A Yale professor of environmental history said, "The courts are still coming around to the necessary role that they may have to play." Just because one court refused to try a case, he added, does not mean that other courts will always do the same.

CLIMATE JUSTICE IN THE WORLD'S COURTROOM

Like the plaintiffs in the *Juliana* case, in May 2019 a group of Torres Strait Islanders made history. They filed the first-ever legal complaint about climate justice with the United Nations. Climate change is destroying their homeland, which is part of Australia, and the islanders claim that the Australian government has not done enough to protect them or the land.

The Torres Strait Islanders are Indigenous People. This means that their ancestors were the earliest known human populations in their part of the world, like the First Nations and Native Peoples of the Americas. The majority of Torres Strait Islanders now live in mainland Australia, but more than four thousand of them still live on their traditional islands.

Those islands lie in a strip of sea called the Torres Strait, between the northern tip of Australia and another large island, Papua New Guinea. More than two hundred fifty islands dot the strait. About fourteen of them are inhabited.

Some of the islands are the rocky tops of underwater mountains. Others, including some inhabited islands, are low-lying, made of coral sand. A number of them rise no more than 3.3 feet (1 meter) above sea level. These islands have already suffered the effects of climate change that you read about in chapter 2. The tropical storms that batter them are becoming more severe. Rising seas slowly creep up their low shorelines, covering or eroding the land. Salt water is contaminating the drinking water. But the damage is not only to the land and water.

"When erosion happens, and the lands get taken away by the seas, it's like a piece of us that gets taken with it—a piece of our heart, a piece of our body. That's why it has an effect on us. Not only the islands but us, as people," says Kabay Tamu, one of the islanders who filed the UN complaint. He is the sixth generation of his family to live on Warraber Island. "We have a sacred site here, which we are connected to spiritually. And disconnecting people from the land, and from the spirits of the land, is devastating."

The future is at risk, Tamu says. "It's devastating to even imagine my grandchildren or my great-grandchildren being forced to leave because of the effects that are out of our hands. We're currently seeing the effects of climate change on our islands daily, with rising seas, tidal surges, coastal erosion and [flooding] of our communities." Torres Strait Islanders fear that, if they are forced to move away from their islands, then their history, culture, and even their language will be lost.

The Torres Strait Islanders are represented in their legal action by a nonprofit group called ClientEarth, which focuses on environmental law. The complaint the group filed with the United Nations Human Rights Committee says that by failing to lower greenhouse gas emissions and take proper measures to protect the islands, the government of Australia has violated the islanders' rights to life, culture, and freedom from interference. ClientEarth said, "Australia is failing its legal human rights obligations to Torres Strait people."

The legal filing also asked the UN committee to tell

Australia to drastically reduce its greenhouse gas emissions and phase out its use of coal. Australia gets about 79 percent of its energy from fossil fuels—coal, oil, and natural gas. The country is a major producer and exporter of coal, which emits higher amounts of carbon dioxide into the atmosphere than other fuels, and which drives climate change.

It will likely take time for the UN committee to answer the Torres Strait Islanders' complaint. As in the case of the complaint brought by Greta Thunberg and other young activists against five countries for their greenhouse gas emissions, the United Nations cannot make Australia do anything, even if the committee rules in favor of the islanders. Member nations must only "consider" what UN committees decide or recommend.

Yet the legal actions at the UN, first by the Torres Strait Islanders and then by Greta Thunberg and other young people, have put climate change—and climate justice—on the world stage. And these legal steps are tools for movements and sympathetic politicians to use in order to demand meaningful action.

No matter how these cases are decided, they are a sign of the changing times. They show that people, including kids, will not sit by while their homelands erode and their futures are darkened to feed the world's addiction to fossil fuels. People have stood up and spoken out to energy companies, governments, courts, and the nations of the world, demanding change. Others will surely follow them. The call for change will become louder as more voices join in, until the resistance is so great that it can no longer be ignored.

WE NEED A
GREEN
JUST TRANSITION
NEW
RIGHT TO
GOOD JOBS
AND A
LIVABLE
FUTURE

PART THREE
WHAT HAPPENS NEXT

CHAPTER 7

CHANGING THE FUTURE

You are going to live with some effects of climate change. So am I. So is my son. So is everyone else.

We can't travel back in time to change the past that got us here—but we can change the future, and we don't need a time machine to do it.

It is impossible to completely avoid climate disruption. The rising temperature of our planet is already changing how people, plants, and animals live, and that will keep happening. Even if the whole world stopped adding any greenhouse gases to the atmosphere tomorrow, temperatures would keep inching up, and the climate would keep changing for some time.

The question we all face is simple: How *much* will it change, and how quickly? How much disruption will we—and the generations that come after us—have to live with?

The answer depends on what we do now. If we follow the lead of young activists like the Torres Strait Islanders, Greta Thunberg, and the *Juliana* plaintiffs, we will greatly lower the amount of greenhouse gases we add to the air. This will bring us to a much brighter climate future than if we keep burning fossil fuels and cutting down forests as if there were no tomorrow. We already know we have to change everything. But how?

People have come up with all kinds of approaches to solving the climate change problem, from the far-out to the practical. Some of these approaches are already in use, but they are not enough by themselves to solve our climate crisis. Other approaches have not yet been tried. Some are risky. Some may not even be possible. But some have already shown that they are keys to a better future.

No single approach will be the best solution in every setting. As you will see in this chapter and the next one, to solve a big, complex problem like worldwide climate change, we can draw on a mix of multiple ideas and tools. They all start, though, with people and their values.

IF CARBON IS THE PROBLEM . . .

If carbon dioxide is driving climate change more than any other greenhouse gas, what about attacking the carbon directly?

That approach has come to be known as carbon capture and storage (CCS). The basic idea behind CCS is that if we suck carbon out of the atmosphere, or keep it from going into the atmosphere, we can put it somewhere safely out of the way, where it can't do any harm.

There are many different versions of CCS. Some of them are still being planned, or are being tested. Others are already in commercial use around the world.

CCS has two main parts. The first part is capturing the carbon. One form of carbon capture is called point-source CCS. This is taking carbon dioxide directly from the sources that produce it, such as power plants that burn fossil fuels, before the gas has a chance to go into the atmosphere. Another form of carbon capture is direct air capture. This is drawing carbon dioxide out of the general atmosphere. It involves fans that move air through filters or chemical devices. Both point-source capture and direct air capture turn the CO_2 into a concentrated stream that can be collected and contained.

A carbon capture facility at a US coal mine.

The second part of CCS is figuring out what to do with the carbon once it has been collected. One solution is to bury it underground and hope it won't find its way out again. Some storage places for CO_2 are seams or spaces in mines or oil fields that have been left empty after coal, oil, or natural gas have been taken out.

Another possibility is to store carbon dioxide in an underground layer of rock. A layer used for carbon storage must have two things. First, it has to be a kind of rock that has a lot of small holes and gaps in it to hold the CO_2. Second, it has to have layers of other, more solid kinds of rock above it. After the CO_2 is pumped down into the more open rock, the solid rock traps it there.

This is the method used at the Sleipner gas field in the North Sea, where a Norwegian company has been mining natural gas and oil from wells since 1974. In 1996 the company started capturing CO_2 from its operations and pumping it into a rock formation about thirty-three thousand feet (a thousand meters) below the seabed. A network of several dozen monitors on the seabed helps test for leaks and disturbances. The British Geological Survey, one of several organizations that has been studying the Sleipner field, reports that "so far, the CO_2 is confined securely within the storage reservoir." Sleipner is considered a successful example of CCS, with the ability to hold many more years' worth of carbon dioxide injections.

A different kind of storage could involve types of rock that bind CO_2. When carbon dioxide comes in contact with these rocks, a chemical reaction takes place that turns the carbon dioxide into part of the rock. In 2013, this approach was tested in Washington State and Iceland. Researchers injected captured carbon dioxide in liquid form into underground basalt, a volcanic rock.

Most of the carbon mineralized—or became solid rock—within two years.

This sounds promising, right? But carbon storage faces a problem. Unless the CO_2 is captured close to where it can be safely injected into the ground, it has to be moved, possibly over long distances. This could be costly, potentially dangerous, and wasteful of the energy needed to transport the CO_2.

The UN Intergovernmental Panel on Climate Change, created to provide governments with the most thorough climate science, has said that carbon capture and storage should play a role in bringing carbon dioxide down to an acceptable level. But there are several reasons CCS isn't going to be close to the whole solution. As of 2019, about thirty million tons of carbon dioxide were captured and stored around the world each year. More than two thirds of the CCS facilities were in North America. Still, the total amount of carbon being captured is a tiny fraction of what is needed to keep us on track for the Paris Agreement target for cutting carbon emissions.

Carbon capture and storage technology is also expensive, and it doesn't make money, which is what companies are formed to do. Companies act in the interests of their profits. While there could be a market for using captured CO_2 to make certain products, energy companies do CCS to get tax benefits from their countries, or to avoid paying pollution penalties. For CCS to have a real impact on climate change, governments—not just corporations—would have to invest more heavily in it. The amount of CCS activity in the world would have to increase enormously.

Beyond cost, though, is the question of safety. Some scientists are concerned about possible problems with carbon storage over long periods of time. We have been using and studying carbon storage for only a few decades. Can we be sure that buried carbon dioxide will never leak into water or air, causing the problem to reappear at a later time? And if we shoot CO_2 into the ground, are we setting the stage for more frequent earth movements and tremors, possibly even earthquakes that would release the stored CO_2? Increased earth movements have been recorded in areas where the fossil-fuel industry uses high-pressure liquids to push oil and gas out of the Earth, in the type of extraction called fracking.

But more than all of this, there is a deeper issue with carbon capture. CCS is simply part of the system that has caused the problem in the first place—the fossil-fuel industry. Building more CCS facilities and moving carbon dioxide around would take a lot of mining and a lot of energy. Where would that energy come from? From fossil fuels like those that probably produced the carbon dioxide in the first place?

Placing our hopes on CCS could encourage us to keep using fossil fuels. We might tell ourselves, "Yes, carbon dioxide emissions are bad, but that doesn't matter because we can clean the air." And this kind of thinking could pull us away from investing in renewable sources of energy, such as solar and wind power, that are cleaner to start with. CCS also puts off the conversation about how much energy we use. In other words, CCS doesn't get to the root of our problem, which is our dependence on fossil fuels, as well as a mindset that tells us we can consume the Earth's resources without limits. It isn't enough to bury the worst by-products of today's crisis while we continue the behavior that caused the crisis in the first place. We should change our behavior so that no one faces the same crisis in the future.

HACKING OUR PLANET

I used to live in a part of British Columbia, Canada, called the Sunshine Coast. That's where my son was born. When he was just three weeks old, my husband and I were up with him at five in the morning when we saw something remarkable through our window. Looking out at the ocean, we spotted two towering black fins—orcas! Then we saw two more.

We had never seen an orca on this part of the coast. Certainly we had never seen one like this, just a few feet from the shore. Seeing four of them felt like a miracle, as if the baby had awakened us to make sure we didn't miss this rare visit.

Later, I learned that a bizarre ocean experiment might have had something to do with our unusual sighting.

In another part of British Columbia, an American businessman named Russ George had dumped 120 tons of iron dust into the ocean from a rented fishing boat. His idea was that the iron would fertilize the ocean and feed algae, creating an algae bloom—a sudden large increase in the number of the tiny plants that float near the surface of the water. Because they are plants, the algae would absorb carbon dioxide from the air. George thought he was demonstrating a way to capture carbon and fight climate change.

George claimed that his ocean experiment created an algae bloom half the size of Massachusetts. It drew sea life from all over the region, including, in his words, whales "counted by the score." Orcas are a type of whale that hunts and feeds on other fish. Were the orcas I saw heading for the all-you-can-eat seafood buffet that had come to feast on George's algae bloom? Probably not, but I couldn't help wondering.

Deliberate interference with Earth's natural systems is called geoengineering, meaning "engineering the Earth." The name suggests that the Earth is a machine that can be tinkered with to get the results we want.

People who want to try geoengineering say that we have already interfered with Earth's systems by spewing greenhouse gases into the air. Why not use our powers of interference to correct that mistake?

Other Worlds?

Elon Musk is a billionaire who founded Tesla, a company that builds electric cars, and SpaceX, a company to launch rockets into space. In 2018 he combined the two in a scientific test that was also a publicity stunt.

SpaceX needed to launch something into space to test its rocket. The object chosen for the test was Musk's own Tesla sports car. He did not ride it into space. The driver's seat was filled by Starman, a mannequin dressed in a space suit. The launch was a success for SpaceX, and Musk's bright-red car now orbits the sun.

One reason Musk has invested in space travel

is that he wants to create a colony on Mars. In his opinion, colonizing Earth's planetary neighbor is necessary to preserve the human race.

Earth may become uninhabitable for humans at some point, Musk fears. Climate disruption could take hold. An asteroid could destroy us all. A devastating world war could turn our home planet into a wasteland. Mars would be our backup plan. A colony there would keep our species from being completely wiped out. Or . . . maybe it would just be cool to go to Mars.

Musk's companies are developing a rocket-and-spaceship combination that he says will carry people to Mars to start a colony there. Experts in planetary science, meanwhile, say that although we could reasonably send humans on scientific missions to Mars at some point, it would be enormously challenging for them to live there permanently. Even if martian colonists solved the huge problems of supplying themselves with air, water, and food, there is another, ever-present danger. No one knows how well our bodies would stand up to long-term exposure to the sun's radiation, both in space and on Mars, where the atmosphere is too thin to block much radiation.

But Elon Musk isn't the only one looking to the stars for a climate change solution. An even more far-fetched idea was mentioned by Rand Paul, a senator from Kentucky, in January 2020. He suggested that we should "begin creating atmospheres on suitable moons or planets."

Making another world livable for humans is called terraforming, from "terra," the Latin word for "land." Turning an alien world into something Earthlike is the subject of a lot of science fiction, but in reality it is a very long way off and may well be impossible.

Paul could have been joking—but the sad fact is that he is one of many politicians who refuse to accept the reality of human-caused climate change. If they don't believe human activity could change Earth's climate, how can they believe we can change the climates of other worlds?

A colony on Mars, or on some other "suitable" moon or planet, even if it were possible, could never be home to the entire human species, because it would be unthinkably costly and difficult to move everyone across space—not to mention all the air, water, and food they would need to survive. At best, a colony on another world could offer a difficult living to a few specially chosen survivors.

Meanwhile, here on Earth, the rest of us can keep our feet on the ground and look for solutions that are really possible. We need to get on with the work of saving the one planet that we know *can* give us life.

Geoengineers call for large-scale actions to cool down the effects of global warming. In addition to schemes to fertilize the ocean, they have come up with ideas for lowering the amount of sunlight that reaches the Earth. Some of these ideas, such as space mirrors to reflect the sun's light away from the planet, are science-fictional and not very practical. Much more attention, though, has been given to the idea of copying certain volcanic eruptions.

Most volcanic eruptions send ash and gases into the lower atmosphere. The gases include a substance called sulfur dioxide. It combines with water vapor in the air to form sulfuric acid. This acid takes the form of an aerosol, a haze of tiny droplets. They simply fall down to Earth. Once in a great while, though, an eruption sends a lot of sulfur dioxide much higher into the atmosphere. Within weeks, air currents carry aerosols around the entire planet.

The droplets act like tiny mirrors, blocking the full heat of the sun from reaching the Earth's surface. As a result, temperatures drop. If such an eruption happens in the tropics, the aerosols can stay in the upper atmosphere for one to two years. They may cause a global cooling that can last even longer.

GEOENGINEERING

Geoengineering schemes include (left to right) placing mirrors in orbit to keep sunlight from reaching the Earth, sending chemicals into the atmosphere to create artificial clouds, and building giant filters to pull greenhouse gases out of the air. Who gets to decide whether the benefits of such schemes outweigh the hazards?

Mount Pinatubo in the Philippines erupted like this in 1991, seeding the upper atmosphere with aerosols. The year after the eruption, global temperatures dropped by half a degree Celsius. Some scientists think that if we could find a way to do with technology what some eruptions do naturally, we could force down the temperature of the Earth and combat global warming.

What could go wrong? Well, the risks of geo-engineering are huge.

Blue skies could become a thing of the past. Depending on what method is used to block the sun, and how much it is used, a permanent haze could cover the Earth. By night, astronomers would have difficulty seeing stars and planets clearly. By day, weaker sunlight could make it harder to produce clean energy from solar power. This is a serious drawback because clean, renewable solar energy is a clear path away from greenhouse gases.

Copying the effects of major volcanic eruptions would likely also change weather and rainfall patterns, with potentially unequal results. Depending on how this type of geoengineering is used, studies have predicted that it could interfere with seasonal rainfall in Asia and Africa, causing drought in some of the world's poorer countries. Geoengineering, in other words, could threaten the food and water sources of billions of people. Climate change itself has already taught us that once we change our planet's atmosphere, many unexpected things can happen.

What about fertilizing the ocean instead—as Russ George did in British Columbia? This type of geoengineering could turn the sea green, but it might do worse things than that. We already know that fertilizer and animal waste that flow into the ocean often trigger "dead zones." These are patches of ocean where there is not enough oxygen in the water to support life.

Fertilizer and waste feed algae blooms, like the one Russ George created off the coast of British Columbia. Algae consume carbon dioxide and release oxygen—which sounds great, at first. But the problem comes from the trillions of tiny ocean creatures and the fish that flock to feed on the algae. They release their own waste into the water. This waste decays, along with dying algae. The process of decay then soaks up more oxygen than the algae released. The result is water that can no longer support many forms of ocean life. Fertilizing the ocean could do more to harm the environment than help it.

Geoengineering—or geohacking, as some call it—also raises questions of fairness. Governments, universities, and private investors or companies are now talking about researching or regulating a range of geoengineering projects. On a large scale, some of these projects could affect the whole world.

Who gets to decide whether or not to dump vast quantities of fertilizers into the sea or shoot aerosols into the sky? Will everyone who might be affected get a vote? What happens if a few countries, or one country, or a single rogue geoengineer decides to go ahead?

In spite of these risks and drawbacks, researchers are working on plans to test various geoengineering schemes. But wouldn't it be better to change our behavior, to reduce our use of fossil fuels, *before* we begin fiddling with our planet's basic life-support systems?

Cutting back on fossil fuels and lowering our emissions of greenhouse gases is something we know will work. It may seem overwhelming to some, because to do it effectively, we really do have to change everything. But isn't that less overwhelming than the changes that will be forced on us if we fail to take well-thought-out action against climate change? Remember too that making a major change in our way of doing things is also our opportunity to create a fairer world for all people and a healthier one for the creatures of our planet's land, sea, and air.

That is a change worth making, and the rest of this chapter shows how some people are already making it. By turning disasters into stepping-stones toward a way of life that fights climate change, they are testing tools that anyone can use and that you and your generation can build on.

AN ANCIENT INVENTION OF NATURE

One form of carbon capture and storage is easy to do, does not require expensive technology, and provides many benefits in addition to cleaning the air.

It is an ancient invention of nature called the tree.

A 2019 article in *Science* magazine called "restoration of trees" on a global scale one of the best ways to limit climate change. The article says that by planting trees to cover 2.2 billion acres (0.9 billion hectares, or slightly less than the total area of the United States) of the Earth's surface—not including the cities, farmland, and forests that already exist—we would increase the forest area of our planet by 25 percent. Once grown, these additional trees could absorb and store a quarter of the carbon in the atmosphere.

There's a catch, though. If we do not act promptly, climate change will make parts of the Earth's surface too hot, dry, or flooded to grow forests.

Other scientists have questioned some of the article's claims, but the overall point is sound. Trees are a powerful weapon against greenhouse gases.

Together with Greta Thunberg, author Philip Pullman, and many other activists, artists, and scientists, I signed a letter about the climate-protecting benefits of trees and other plants that was published online in 2019. You can read it at the back of this book under the heading

"A Natural Solution to the Climate Disaster." In the letter, we urged the world's governments to work with local communities on "a thrilling but neglected approach to averting climate chaos while defending the living world."

Ecosystems are our planet's natural tools for taking excess carbon out of the air, because the plants in every ecosystem absorb CO_2 and release oxygen. Not just forests but also wetlands, grasslands, marshes, and even natural seabeds remove and store carbon. They are also home to many of the living things that share our planet and now face mass extinction because of our activities. Our goal should be to protect, restore, and grow these vital ecosystems while we work to make our industries and our way of life less dependent on carbon.

This is something we can do right now. It would be wonderful if the world joined in a huge tree-planting project, but until it does, we can act on our own, in whatever patches of earth we have. Trees are homes for birds and insects, sources of food (certain kinds of trees, at least), and symbols of belief in the future, because they take a long time to grow. Planting and tending even a single tree says, "I believe in that future too."

LIGHTING THE WAY

A powerful hurricane struck Puerto Rico in September

2017. Hurricane Maria lashed the Caribbean island, which is part of the United States, with high winds and heavy rain. After the storm's fury died down, people left their homes to take stock of the damage.

In the small mountain city of Adjuntas, they found themselves without electricity and water. This was true across Puerto Rico. But Adjuntas was also totally cut off from the rest of the island. Every single road was blocked by mounds of mud that had washed down from the peaks, or by tangles of fallen trees and branches.

There was one bright spot in Adjuntas, though. Just off the main square, light shone through every window of a large pink house. The building glowed like a beacon in the terrifying darkness.

What I saw in Puerto Rico after the hurricane reminded me in many ways of what I had seen in New Orleans after Hurricane Katrina. But one part of the island, that shining pink house, felt very different. I soon learned that something new and hopeful was happening around it.

That house was Casa Pueblo, a community center and the headquarters of an environmental group. Twenty years earlier, a family of scientists and engineers had founded Casa Pueblo. On its roof they had put solar panels, which capture the sun's energy and turn it into electricity. At that time, solar panels may have seemed like a futuristic or fringe thing to do. But over the years Casa Pueblo had upgraded its panels and made use of the island's plentiful sunshine.

Unlike the electrical poles that were down across the island, those solar panels had somehow survived the winds and falling trees of Hurricane Maria. In the sea of darkness after the storm, Casa Pueblo had the only lasting electrical power for miles around.

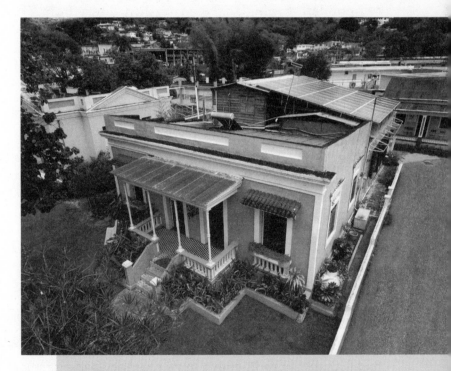

Casa Pueblo's rooftop solar panels made the pink building a beacon in the darkness after Hurricane Maria ravaged Puerto Rico.

People from all over the hills of Adjuntas made their way to the warm and welcoming light. It would be weeks before the official disaster-relief agencies would bring significant help, so the community organized its own relief efforts. The pink house quickly became the nerve center. People gathered food and water, tarps to make temporary shelters, and chain saws to clear the streets. They used the priceless supply of solar power to charge their phones.

Casa Pueblo also became a lifesaving field hospital. Elderly people who needed electricity to power their oxygen machines filled its airy rooms. Thanks to its solar panels, the center's radio station could keep broadcasting. The storm had knocked out power lines and cell towers, so that station was the community's only source of information.

I arrived in Puerto Rico a few months into these efforts. I had come to see how this US territory was dealing with the disaster. I visited the island's south coast, home to a lot of their industry. People there had suffered some of Maria's most cruel effects. Their low-lying neighborhoods were flooded. They feared that the storm had stirred up toxic chemicals from nearby power plants and other industries. And even though the area had two of the island's largest electricity plants, many people were still living in the dark.

Later that day, the bleak mood shifted as we drove up into the mountains to Casa Pueblo. Open doors welcomed us. We drank coffee from the center's own coffee plantation, which the community manages. Overhead, rain drummed on those precious solar panels. It was like stepping through a portal into another world—a Puerto Rico where everything worked and the mood was hopeful.

Now those solar panels didn't look silly at all. In fact, they looked like the best hope for survival in a future that is sure to bring more drastic weather shocks like Hurricane Maria—a storm that had been supercharged by climate change.

THE BATTLE FOR PARADISE

The rising temperatures of global warming made Hurricane Maria extra powerful, but long before those fierce winds came, Puerto Rico had other problems.

Puerto Rico is not a state. It's a colony of the United States. That means its people do not have the same rights as other Americans. They cannot vote in federal elections, and the federal government generally treats the island as a way to make money for the mainland.

Also, because it is a colony, Puerto Rico did not design its own economy. The island imports 85 percent of its food, even though it has some of the most fertile soil in the world. Before Maria, it also got 98 percent of its energy from imported fossil fuels, even though it has sun, wind, and waves that could provide plenty of cheap, clean, renewable power. There were many other ways that Puerto Rico's economy had been built to serve others, and for that reason, it had accumulated large debts, owed to a range of creditors off the island.

A new chapter in the island's troubles began in 2016, when a US law created a program that brought new economic suffering. The law claimed that it would make Puerto Rico's debt more manageable and speed up infrastructure and development projects on the island. In reality, it attacked the glue that holds a society together: education, health care, the electricity and water systems, communications networks, and more—all to cut costs and pay off creditors.

It's no wonder the law didn't help Puerto Ricans. It put an unelected board of managers in charge of overseeing the territory's economy. To free up funds toward paying Puerto Rico's debts, this board approved an austerity plan that slashed the budget for public services. The economic program simply made Puerto Rico's bad situation worse. And then Hurricane Maria roared through.

The storm was so powerful that it would have made

even the sturdiest society reel. Puerto Rico didn't just reel. It broke.

About three thousand people lost their lives as a result of Hurricane Maria. A few were lost to the raging wind and water. Most deaths, though, happened afterward. People could not plug in medical equipment when electricity was down for months. Some had no choice but to drink contaminated water. Health networks did not have medicine to treat illnesses. These tragedies showed how all levels of government entrusted to protect Puerto Ricans, on the island and in Washington, DC, had failed to put in place sturdy systems for supplying essential services in emergencies.

Hurricane Katrina had exposed the same weaknesses in emergency preparation and disaster response in New Orleans. And now, in Puerto Rico, similar problems unfolded long after the disaster itself.

Along with smashing the island's infrastructure, Maria damaged its supply lines for food and fuel. And just as things had been after Hurricane Katrina in New Orleans twelve years earlier, federal emergency relief efforts failed horribly in Puerto Rico. A contract to supply thirty million meals to Puerto Rico went to a Georgia company that had a record of failure and a staff of one person. A Montana energy company with just two employees (and ties to the US secretary of the Interior) got a $300 million contract to help rebuild the energy grid. These contracts were later canceled, but because of these and other failures, desperately needed food supplies and electrical repair materials sat unused in warehouses for months.

So, long after the storm, ordinary Puerto Ricans were still living by flashlight and battling depression and misery because once again, the government had used a disaster as an opportunity to hand out corporate contracts.

Like Hurricane Katrina in New Orleans, the catastrophe of Maria was more than a natural disaster. It was a storm supercharged by climate change that slammed into a society that had been deliberately weakened by government decisions. Those decisions had given greater weight to debt repayment than to the well-being of people and their communities.

The limp, late relief efforts after the storm showed how little those in power valued the lives of Americans who were largely poor, Spanish speaking, and descended from slaves and Indigenous People. Communities in Florida and Texas, however, received more and faster aid after similar devastating hurricanes that year.

But even though the story of Hurricane Maria seemed to be just another sadly familiar cycle of neglect, crisis, and disaster capitalism, there is hope. After Maria, Puerto Rico became more than a disaster scene. It also became a battleground of ideas. On one side were the usual disaster capitalists, treating Puerto Rico the way they had treated New Orleans. On the other side were Puerto Ricans struggling to survive, but also doing things differently.

Casa Pueblo, the light in the darkness after the storm, shows a path that could take Puerto Ricans—and others around the world—to a more secure future.

Fighting for Hearts and Minds

For one activist from Bayamón, Puerto Rico, environmental passion started at an early age. Amira C. Odeh Quiñones remembers snorkeling at a coral reef when she was six years old. By the time she was twelve, she says, "It no longer existed."

Odeh Quiñones was in her midtwenties in 2017, when Hurricane Maria struck Puerto Rico. "I saw all of the destruction and how much we depended on imports because when the ports closed for some days we would run out of food," she says. "The streets I walked all my life were unrecognizable. It was scary to see that after each day that passed nothing got better."

To focus on social and climate justice after Maria, Odeh Quiñones organized a branch of 350.org, a group that describes itself as "an international movement of ordinary people working to end the age of fossil fuels and build a world of community-led renewable energy for all." (I was on its board of directors for many years.) In addition, her environmental work has included a successful campaign to stop the sale of bottled water on the campus of the University of Puerto Rico.

Beyond the issue of climate change, Odeh Quiñones wants to see justice for the people of Puerto Rico, as the island struggles to recover from Hurricane Maria. The lasting damage from the storm, she points out, has ruined lives. "The coastal communities or mountain towns still have thousands of homes destroyed," she says. "Not only is there still broken infrastructure but also broken families. . . . The recovery of the minds and hearts haven't happened at all."

Decision-making about Puerto Rico's future, claims Odeh Quiñones, should include all of its people. "Communities should be in this conversation because whatever policy is decided will be key for us to be able to survive." She is right. Solutions are more likely to be accepted and to work when the people who will live with them have the chance to help shape them, rather than people being told from above or from outside what they must do. Whether in the aftermath of a hurricane or in the face of climate change, those who are most affected must be heard.

LEARNING FROM CASA PUEBLO

On a tour of Casa Pueblo, I saw the solar-powered radio station and the solar-powered movie theater that had opened after the storm. There was a butterfly garden and a store that sold local crafts as well as Casa Pueblo's popular coffee. Pictures on the wall showed scenes from the forest school where the center does outdoor education. They also showed a protest in Washington, DC, that had stopped a project to build a gas pipeline through the mountains near Casa Pueblo.

Arturo Massol-Deyá, a biologist, and president of Casa Pueblo's board of directors, told me that the hurricane had changed his view of what was possible. For years he had pushed for Puerto Rico to get more of its energy from renewable sources, such as solar panels and wind turbines. With the island depending on imported fossil fuel, and a few centralized stations producing power, he had warned that one big storm could knock out the whole electrical grid.

Then it happened.

Now, after the storm, everyone understood the risks Massol-Deyá had spoken of. The collapse of the old system was helping him make the case for renewable energy. But even solar panels and wind turbines can be damaged in storms. This can be a problem if power comes from huge, central solar and wind farms that send electricity long distances over lines that can be blown down. Instead, people began to understand, a system of small, community-based power systems, like Casa Pueblo's, can produce electricity right where it is used.

To spread the word about the benefits of solar power, Casa Pueblo handed out fourteen thousand solar lanterns after the storm. These small boxes sit outside during the day, taking in and storing the sun's energy. By night they create pools of light.

The center also distributed solar-powered refrigerators to households that still lacked power months after the storm. Casa Pueblo has now started a campaign that calls for half of Puerto Rico's power to come from the sun.

Several Puerto Ricans I spoke with called Hurricane Maria "our teacher." The storm taught people what didn't work. It also taught them what *did* work—not just solar panels but also small organic farms that used traditional farming methods, which stood up to floods and wind better than modern industrial farming. And unlike imported food, products from local farms were available even when long-distance transport was interrupted.

Overnight, everyone could see just how dangerous it was for this fertile island to have lost control over its agricultural system. But in communities that still had traditional farms, people could also see that the old, ecologically aware way of farming was not some quaint relic of the past. It was a crucial tool for surviving the future.

The storm showed the importance of deep community relationships, including ties to Puerto Ricans who were living off the island. When the government kept failing, people managed to give lifesaving aid to each other.

After Maria, dozens of Puerto Rican organizations came together to demand change. Under the banner *Junte Gente* (Spanish for "The People Together"), they call for a fair and just shift to the next, rebuilt economy. They want that economy to be based on community; clean energy; and new education, transportation, and food systems that truly serve the Puerto Rican people—not just a reinforced copy of the old system.

Disasters such as hurricanes disrupt ordinary life. Often, rebuilding a community or even a country is necessary after a disaster. As you saw in chapter 3, some people see these disruptions and reconstructions as opportunities to make the rich richer. But the rebuilding after a disaster can go in the opposite direction. It can be an opportunity to enact good ideas that were once seen as impossible. It can be an opportunity to change the old, harmful ways we have been doing things—and a chance to plan a future that can better cope with the shocks of climate change, as well as other crises like pandemics.

GREENING GREENSBURG

Like Puerto Rico, the town of Greensburg, Kansas, was devastated by a disaster. Unlike Puerto Rico, the town had political independence and received the financial aid it needed, not just to rebuild itself but to reinvent itself as a town looking toward the future, not the past.

On a May night in 2007, Greensburg was nearly wiped off the map by a tornado. It was no ordinary storm—it was big and powerful enough to be called a super-tornado. Its winds reached tearing speeds of 205 miles (330 kilometers) per hour. Where it touched the ground, it was about 1.7 miles (2.7 kilometers) across, wider than the town itself.

People who live in Kansas know about tornadoes. When the warning sirens sounded in Greensburg that night, the residents took cover in basements or the most secure places they could find. For customers at a gas station store, for example, the safest place was inside the walk-in cooler.

The tornado was preceded by lightning and a hail of large ice pellets. Then the funnel cloud moved slowly across the town. When it was over, 95 percent of the buildings in Greensburg were destroyed or damaged. Eleven people were dead. Sixty more were injured.

Afterward, about half the town's 1,500 or so people moved away. Those who remained held meetings in tents to discuss rebuilding their community.

"The number one topic at those tent meetings was talking about who we are—what are our values? . . . Sometimes we agreed to disagree, but we were still civil to each other," said Bob Dixson, Greensburg's mayor at the time. Like many other people who lived in the rural area, Dixson had roots in a long line of farmers. He added, "Let's not forget that our ancestors were stewards of the land. My ancestors lived in the original green homes: sod houses. . . . We learned that the only true green and sustainable things in life are how we treat each other."

So Greensburg decided to reinvent itself as an

environmentally friendly green town. With the help of government disaster-relief grants, nonprofit organizations, and a local business that built a big wind turbine, Greensburg became a model of sustainable living.

Its new public buildings meet the high standards of the LEED (Leadership in Energy and Environmental Design) rating system, a program that certifies the environmental friendliness of buildings. The LEED rating system measures features such as whether a building is placed on a site in the best way for the local environment, whether it uses energy and water efficiently, and whether it is made from sustainable materials that are produced or harvested without destroying limited resources. Half a dozen of Greenburg's structures, including the community's new hospital and school, have LEED's highest-level platinum certification.

Students were part of this planning process. They had ideas about their new school, and they did not hesitate to share them. One of the architects who worked with the town on the rebuilding said, "If not for the outspoken input of the youth, the school would be an ordinary regional school located ten miles from town on a site the school board purchased within a week of the storm. But because the next generation saw a need for change and had the desire to stand up for it, the school is now an anchor for the community sited along Main Street, both transforming education and adding vitality to the community."

Clean, renewable energy powers the town. Most of it comes from wind. The force of nature that nearly ended Greensburg now turns large and small turbines that power businesses, public buildings, and farms.

This bold reinvention has benefited the town in several ways. One benefit is the money its renewable energy sources have saved. The hospital spends 59 percent less on energy than a typical hospital of its size, and the school saves 72 percent. Another benefit is that the town is likely to fare better if another tornado comes along. Houses and apartments are being built using methods, such as having straw bales in their walls, that not only save energy but may strengthen those structures against high winds.

Although Greensburg's population remains smaller than before the tornado, the little town's influence is big. The story of Greensburg's greening has been told in books, articles, two documentary miniseries, and the halls of Congress. Planners from other parts of the country, as well as young people learning about environmentally sustainable living, come to the town to see how it's done.

The Big Well in Greensburg, Kansas, called "the world's largest hand-dug well," is 109 feet (33 meters) deep. It survived the 2007 tornado that nearly wiped out the town, but the museum around it was destroyed. Today the rebuilt museum—whose new staircase echoes the tornado's spiral shape—chronicles Greensburg's rebirth as a green town.

Greensburg showed the power of shared decision-making at the community level. It showed that people who suffered a terrible loss had the courage to start over in a new way that looks toward the future. Another lesson from Greensburg is the power and efficiency of thinking big. If individuals had rebuilt their homes and businesses with energy-efficient windows and appliances, those changes would have been good. But by thinking on a bigger scale and imagining a whole new kind of town, the people of Greensburg were able to get the support and funding needed to make a much bigger difference in the fight against climate change.

What if there was a way to help many towns and cities become more like Greensburg, but without waiting for disasters to smash them first? What if we had a plan to take the lessons of Casa Pueblo nationwide, or worldwide?

Read on—there is a way.

CHAPTER 8

A GREEN NEW DEAL

The world's climate scientists have told us what we must do in order to bring the warming of our planet under control. We'll have to change almost everything about how we get energy, use resources, and live. Does a change that big sound impossible?

It isn't. We've done it before, more than once. And we did it at times when the nation and the world were in crisis, just as the world is in a climate and economic crisis today.

THE ORIGINAL NEW DEAL

A sweeping change happened in the United States during

the 1930s. Under President Franklin D. Roosevelt, the country launched dozens of programs that changed government and the economy. Together these programs were called the New Deal.

The background to the New Deal was an economic catastrophe called the Great Depression. In the United States, it started in October 1929. The flow of money from investors on the stock exchange had driven prices of many stocks—which are shares of ownership in corporations and financial funds—to high values. Investments of this type can create economic instability because they are always subject to cycles of rising and falling. This time, people panicked at reports that stocks were overpriced and due to lose value. Nervous investors happened to sell a huge number of shares in just one week. The value of shares dropped suddenly and dramatically, sending shock waves through the economy.

Banks failed. Businesses closed. Millions of people lost their jobs. Most of those who still had jobs suffered sharp cuts in pay. Government felt the pinch too, because its income from taxes quickly went down. As international trade weakened and then collapsed, the economic depression spread to other countries.

Never had the United States known such widespread poverty, suffering, and hunger. Shantytowns sprang up.

People who could no longer pay rent or find work made what shelters they could out of scrap wood, old cloth, and cardboard. They roamed the nation's cities, towns, and countryside, looking for work or begging for food. Black Americans were hardest hit. They were the first to lose their jobs, and they were unemployed at higher rates than whites.

At first, the government did little to help. No federal programs existed to provide a social safety net that could support unemployed people or those who were elderly or disabled.

But after Roosevelt became president in 1933, he promised to offer Americans a "new deal." To combat the misery and breakdown of the Great Depression, his administration launched a flurry of new policies, programs, and public investments. Minimum wage laws were introduced to protect workers from being grossly underpaid. Social Security was created to give older people a source of income after their working lives and to help people who were disabled and could not work.

Because a major cause of the Great Depression was reckless behavior by banks that had used their customers' money to make risky investments in stocks, or to lend money to companies in which bank officials owned stocks, an important piece of the New Deal was new regulations to keep banks from such behavior in the future. An Emergency Banking Act allowed banks to reopen, but under federal oversight. These strict federal regulations were understood to be necessary for the overall health of the economy—just as scientists now urge strict regulation of greenhouse gas emissions for the overall health of the planet.

Other New Deal programs brought electricity to most of rural America for the first time and built a wave of low-cost housing in cities. In the center of the country, where drought had turned vast stretches of farmland into a Dust Bowl, agricultural aid focused on protecting soil. These programs helped the country recover from the Depression by creating jobs and protecting people's livelihoods.

One way the New Deal attacked unemployment was with a program called the Civilian Conservation Corps (CCC). This organization was created to provide work for young men, including

Young men clean up at the "wash room" of a Civilian Conservation Corps camp in California's Eastern Sierra range in 1933. The CCC was part of the New Deal that lifted America out of the Great Depression.

older teens. Volunteers had to sign up for at least six months. They were fed, housed in work camp dormitories, and paid a small monthly salary—most of which they were supposed to send home to help support their families. Thousands of them were taught to read and write, or acquired new job skills, during their time in the CCC.

In exchange for these benefits, the volunteers worked on public projects, mostly outdoors and in the West. The benefits to the environment were extensive. Volunteers planted more than 2.3 billion trees during the life of the CCC. They built or improved roads, bridges, flood-control levees and dams, and other structures. Many projects were located in America's national and state parks, including the eight hundred new parks the CCC helped to create. Large numbers of these structures can still be seen today.

At its peak in 1935, the CCC had half a million volunteers in twenty-nine hundred camps. As many as three million American men passed through the CCC during the nine years of the program. African American men could take part, but the camps were segregated by race. Women could not join, except at one camp, where they learned canning and other household tasks.

Other New Deal programs left a lasting legacy across

the United States. The Works Progress Administration employed people to build schools, roads, airports, and more.

In all, more than thirty new agencies were created between 1933 and 1940, and the government directly employed more than ten million people.

The biggest shortcoming of the New Deal was that it overwhelmingly favored white, male workers. Women, Black people, Mexican Americans, and Indigenous Peoples benefited less. Still, the New Deal showed that a society can make huge changes within just ten years. The New Deal expressed a shift in values. The focus moved from wealth and profits at all costs to helping others and rebuilding a more secure economy and society.

Along with the shift in values came swift changes in government responsibilities and federal spending. To cope with an urgent crisis, the government acted quickly and brought about a big transformation. When people today say that there isn't enough money to pay for the changes needed to fight climate change, or that a government or an economy can't move that fast, the New Deal reminds us that there *is*, and it *can*.

During the New Deal, not everything was paid for by the federal government with taxpayers' dollars. Roosevelt's administration created insurance and loan programs that encouraged banks and individuals to invest in the economy. A mix of government and private money paid for the New Deal, which pulled millions of families out of poverty. The same thing can happen today—and without the New Deal's racial and gender exclusions—if we decide to change everything.

Young People in the New Deal

"I live in real terror when I think we may be losing this generation," said Eleanor Roosevelt in 1934. "We have got to bring these young people into the active life of the community and make them feel that they are necessary."

The wife of President Franklin D. Roosevelt felt that her husband's New Deal was not doing enough for young people. Many young men and women could not find work. Others could not afford to stay in college. Together with educators, Eleanor Roosevelt pushed for a program especially for them.

The result was the National Youth Administration (NYA), created in 1935. The NYA granted money to high school and college students in exchange for part-time work. This let the students stay in school without borrowing money or leaving school to seek jobs. For example, one young man in Idaho taught classes at the local YMCA in exchange for an NYA grant that allowed him to stay in school at a junior college.

For young people who were not in school but could not find jobs, the NYA offered on-the-job training in federal work programs. It later changed its focus to teaching job skills such as sewing and auto repair to young people.

After the United States entered World War II, young men and women learned skills related to national defense. The NYA trained girls to operate X-ray machines in hospitals, to use machine tools such as drills in an aircraft manufacturing plant, and to assemble radios.

The makers of the original New Deal created the NYA because they saw that they could not ignore young people. As with today's young people, they refused to be overlooked. Your generation will be part of whatever changes we make to tackle the problems of climate change and injustice. And just as the young people of the New Deal found a way to use their skills or learned new ones, you'll see in the next chapter that the skills you already have, or new skills you gain, can be a valuable part of your activism.

A MARSHALL PLAN FOR THE EARTH

The New Deal was not the only time in modern history when people met drastic challenges with rapid, large-scale action. During World War II (1939–1945), Western nations changed their industries overnight to fight Hitler's Germany. Factories that had made consumer products such as washing machines and cars switched with astonishing speed to making ships, planes, and weapons.

People changed their lifestyles, too. To free up fuel for the military, they stopped or reduced their driving. In Britain, there was virtually no driving for anything that wasn't truly necessary. North Americans also drove much less. Between 1938 and 1944, use of public transit such as buses and trains went up by 95 percent in Canada and went up by 87 percent in the United States.

People grew their own food in their yards or community plots to free up agricultural crops for the military. In 1943, twenty million American households had "victory gardens." This meant that three-fifths of the nation's population were growing fresh vegetables.

Then, when the war ended, western and southern Europe were left in a ravaged state. Economies were ruined. So were many cities and landscapes.

US Secretary of State George C. Marshall convinced Congress that the United States should help rebuild the nations of Europe—including Germany, the chief enemy during the war. He argued that there would be long-term benefits to the United States and to capitalism. A recovering Europe would provide a growing market for US products.

In April 1948, Congress agreed to what came to be called the Marshall Plan. Spending for the plan eventually totaled more than $12 billion, the largest aid program in the country's history to that point. Aid began with shipments of food, fuel, and medical supplies. The next stage was investment in rebuilding power plants, factories, schools, and railways.

The Marshall Plan did much to put European factories, businesses, schools, and social programs back on their feet. And, as Marshall had predicted, by lifting up the stricken nations of Europe, the United States helped itself, too. It forged stronger trade and political ties to those nations, which were ready to engage in international commerce much sooner than they would have been without the Marshall Plan.

Today, with the climate crisis upon us, some people have called for a global or green Marshall Plan for the world. One of the first to talk about it was Angélica Navarro Llanos.

I met Navarro Llanos in 2009. At the time she was

representing the South American nation of Bolivia at international meetings. She had just made a speech to a United Nations climate conference, in which she said:

> *Millions of people in small islands, least-developed countries, landlocked countries as well as vulnerable communities in Brazil, India and China, and all around the world— are suffering from the effects of a problem to which they did not contribute. . . . We need a Marshall Plan for the Earth . . . to ensure we reduce emissions while raising people's quality of life.*

A Marshall Plan for the Earth could be a way for the wealthier, longer-industrialized nations to pay their climate debt to the rest of the world, as discussed in chapter 3. In addition to transforming their own economies by shifting away from fossil fuels to renewable energy, those wealthier nations could provide resources for the rest of the world to do the same thing. This could also pull huge swaths of humanity out of poverty and provide people with services, such as electricity and clean water, that they now lack.

If we are to prepare the world to face and fight climate

change, we must start by calling a halt to new coal mines, offshore rigs for drilling oil, and fracking new fields of oil and gas. But beyond that, we have to cut down and eventually halt our use of the mines, drilling rigs, and fracking fields that already exist. At the same time, while we reduce our use of fossil fuels—and also reduce our greenhouse gas emissions from other activities such as industrial agriculture—we have to rapidly increase our use of renewable energy and ecological farming methods, so that we can get our global carbon emissions down to zero by the middle of this century.

The good news is that we can do all of this with the tools and technology we already have. More good news: we can create hundreds of millions of good jobs around the world as we move from an economy based on fossil fuels to an economy without carbon emissions. Jobs would open up in many kinds of work:

- designing, making, and installing renewable energy technology such as solar panels and wind turbines

- building and operating public transit such as high-speed electric trains, to provide good alternatives to much driving and flying

- cleaning polluted land and water, restoring damaged wildlife habitat and wilderness areas, and planting trees

- upgrading homes, businesses, factories, and public buildings to make them more energy-efficient

- teaching children, providing mental health support, caring for the sick and elderly, and making art—all of which are already low-carbon professions and can be made even more so with the right adjustments.

Would programs like these be expensive? Yes, but the New Deal and the Marshall Plan proved that governments can find resources when they have to. More recently, the US government spent enormous sums bailing out bankrupt financial institutions and buoying up the economy after a financial crisis and recession in 2008–2009 and again amid the COVID-19 economic downturn. The money is there—if the need is clear and people demand it.

And the need for climate action *is* clear. People and movements across the United States and around the world are calling for their governments to meet the climate crisis with sweeping programs of changes.

The forces that are failing us are our dependence on fossil fuels, the power of international energy and agribusiness corporations, and the stranglehold of business as usual. They are not just destroying our planet. They are destroying people's quality of life.

People are hurt by the growing gap between the ultra-rich and everyone else; by the trampling on the rights of poor and Indigenous People; and by the crumbling of bridges, dams, and other public works; just as much as by the effects of climate change. Can our current economic system be relied on to change this? Unlikely. The rise of free-market ideas has weakened the notion that governments are responsible for regulating what corporations can do. And without regulations, corporations have no reason to act against their own interest—which is profit.

To make the deep transformation that is needed to ensure our best future, we need a plan that tackles climate change *and* reforms the economic model that drives it. We could have societies and economies that are built to protect and renew our planet's life-support systems while also respecting and supporting all of us who depend on those systems.

Making a change this big and this broad is a huge

task. As with the New Deal, the World War II effort, and the Marshall Plan, new laws and regulations will be needed to bring about a massive transformation. Governments will have to change their spending habits to pay for it. People have developed a number of visions of this transformation. To highlight the fact that we already have an example in our history, most of them are called a Green New Deal.

THE GREEN NEW DEAL—AND MORE

Young climate activists from a group called the Sunrise Movement made news in late 2018 when they held sit-ins at the office of the soon-to-be Speaker of the US House of Representatives. The youth-led movement felt that leaders of government were not doing enough about the climate crisis, so they brought the crisis to the government.

Even members of the Sunrise Movement who were too young to vote took a passionate interest in politics. They urged political candidates to refuse donations from the fossil-fuel industry. They supported candidates who favored renewable energy.

Above all, the young people of the Sunrise Movement called on political leaders to plan a Green New Deal. Such a plan would end the country's dependence on

Today's young people join the call for a Green New Deal to build a livable future.

fossil fuels while also creating environmentally safe jobs and guaranteeing social and climate justice.

The idea of an environmental version of the New Deal has been around since the mid-2000s. Economists, environmentalists, and a few politicians raised the idea in the United States and Great Britain and at the United Nations. In the fall of 2018, though, it became a mainstream political issue after the UN Intergovernmental

Panel on Climate Change released its report detailing the actions needed to meet the goal of keeping global warming below 1.5°C (2.7°F) by 2100, as discussed in chapter 2.

In early 2019, Congresswoman Alexandria Ocasio-Cortez and Senator Ed Markey presented one possible plan to the US Congress as a Green New Deal resolution.

The resolution asked Congress to commit to moving the nation toward zero carbon emissions and commit to a goal of getting all energy from clean, renewable sources very rapidly. Ways to do this would include:

- upgrading existing buildings, and constructing new ones to make efficient use of energy and water

- supporting clean manufacturing practices, such as switching to different raw materials and techniques that would reduce pollution and greenhouse gases from industry and manufacturing

- investing in more efficient power grids and working to make electricity affordable and clean

- overhauling the nation's transportation
  system, including investing in public
  transportation, high-speed trains, and vehicles
  that do not emit greenhouse gases.

The version of the Green New Deal offered by Ocasio-Cortez and Markey had goals that went beyond cutting carbon, into the realm of improving society through wide-reaching changes. It wanted guarantees that all Americans would be provided with jobs that pay enough to support a family; with education, including college; with high-quality health care; with safe, affordable housing; and with "access to clean water, clean air, healthy and affordable food, and nature." It stressed that all these things were rights, not privileges, and should never be denied to people simply because they lack money.

This Green New Deal aimed at putting the ideals of fairness and justice into practice, as well as fighting climate change. The benefits would go far beyond limiting climate change. Jobs and environmental protection would receive a huge, lifesaving boost. Systems that lock in inequalities and injustices—between Black and white people, between citizens and immigrants, between women and men, between Indigenous People and non-Indigenous people—would start to crumble.

The resolution presented by Senator Markey and Representative Ocasio-Cortez did not pass in a Senate vote. But a number of US senators and representatives support some form of a Green New Deal, although some of them want to focus only on environmental and climate solutions. And public pressure for progress on climate change is not going away. Another Green New Deal proposal will come before Congress before long.

People and political parties are calling for similar plans in other countries too. In Canada, Australia, the European Union, the United Kingdom, and other nations, voters and leaders will be asked to choose: commit to some version of a Green New Deal, or let "business as usual" keep adding carbon to the atmosphere.

When we do adopt a Green New Deal, we must avoid things that have failed us in the past. We must make sure that no one is excluded or left behind because they lack political power. We must recognize that when it comes to climate change, business interests are not the same as the interests of the people and the planet. We must not let corporate and business interests make all the decisions, although we must also work to sustain our economies, including businesses that want to be part of the solution. We must seek deep change based in shared, democratic decision-making, with all of our voices heard.

We need more than a New Deal painted green, or a Marshall Plan with solar panels.

Instead of the New Deal's highly centralized dams and fossil-fuel power plants, we need wind and solar power that is produced by many sources and, where possible, owned by communities.

Instead of sprawling white suburbs and racially segregated inner-city housing projects, we need beautifully designed, racially integrated, zero-carbon sustainable urban housing, built with input from communities of color, rather than shaped entirely by real estate developers and investors whose only goal is profit.

Instead of handing over conservation of our natural resources and public lands to military and federal agencies, we need to empower Indigenous communities, small farmers and ranchers, and folk who practice sustainable fishing. They can lead a process of planting billions of trees, repairing wetlands, and renewing soil and reefs.

In other words, we need things we've never tried on a large scale. We need to build society around the understanding that well-being for all matters more than economic growth. Only then can we truly move away from climate-changing pollution and climate injustice.

Another thing we haven't yet tried is paying the climate debt you read about in chapter 3. This would benefit the whole world by helping poorer nations cut their carbon emissions and advance toward clean energy.

We could also try rejecting a way of life that centers on shopping. The world does not have enough resources and energy to give everyone a life of consumer luxury. We could, though, improve everyone's quality of life in different ways.

The United States and many other societies have become trapped in the belief that "quality of life" means working harder, consuming more and more things, and gaining wealth. But if that were really making us happy, would we see such high levels of stress, depression, and substance abuse? What if the economy were set up for people to work less, so that they would have more time for friendship, recreation, being in nature, and making and enjoying art? Research has shown that these things—which demand far less energy and fewer resources than the constant stream of manufactured consumer objects—really do make people happier.

More than anything else, the health of our planet will determine the quality of all our lives. When hundreds of chanting young members of the Sunrise Movement lined the halls of Congress, they wore shirts that read WE HAVE A RIGHT TO A LIVABLE FUTURE AND GOOD JOBS. They held banners that read WE HAVE 12 YEARS. WHAT IS YOUR

PLAN? And they offered much more than criticism of the problems. They offered a story about what the world could look like after a deep change, and they offered a plan for how to get there.

The climate movement is good at saying no—no to pollution and no to more drilling and extraction. The Green New Deal is something different. It's a big, bold yes to go along with those no's. It doesn't just tell us what we can't do. It shows us what we can do instead.

Your generation is spreading the vision of a Green New Deal. Young people are telling us that politicians can no longer avoid it, and they are right.

Buen Vivir, Living Well Together

If we turn away from the idea that nature is a thing to be conquered and depleted by humans, what ideas will take its place? Is there a different way to view the world and our place in it?

There is. One example is *buen vivir*, a Spanish expression for "living well." Social movements in Ecuador and Bolivia use it to mean "living well together." *Buen vivir* is a view of life rooted in the beliefs of Indigenous Peoples in those South American countries. It promotes harmonious relationships—not just harmony among individuals but harmony between people and the natural world. *Buen vivir* respects cultures, shared community values, and other living things. It sees humans as living in partnership with the land and its resources, not as their owners or masters.

Buen vivir is about the right to a good life, where everyone has enough, instead of the more-and-more life of constant consumerism. Movements across South America are taking *buen vivir* as a starting point for talking about social, economic, and environmental issues.

A victory in New Zealand reflects the values of *buen vivir*, even though it was won across the Pacific Ocean from South America.

The Maori are the Indigenous People in what is now called New Zealand. In 2017, after more than a century of petitions and legal actions, Maori people who live along the Whanganui River won legal "personhood" for the river. The New Zealand government officially recognized that the river nourishes the Maori, both physically and spiritually. It guaranteed the river the same rights in law as a person or a corporation. This act opened up new possibilities for expressing our values, protecting the natural world, and changing the way we interact with it.

MIGHTY MOVEMENTS

As we develop a vision for a Green New Deal, climate and justice activists today can learn valuable lessons from the original New Deal and the Marshall Plan. One lesson is that it is always possible to find a new approach to a crisis. In the 1930s the United States faced the emergency of economic depression and unemployment. In the 1940s and into the 1950s, it faced the disaster of European and Asian countries that had been broken by war.

What happened in each case? Entire societies—consumers, workers, manufacturers, and every level of government—were part of the response. Many parts of society came together to bring about deep change. They shared clear goals: to rescue the economy by creating jobs for unemployed people during the Depression, and to lift up a continent crushed by World War II.

Another lesson is that the problem solvers of the past did not look for only a single answer to the problem. And they did not simply tinker with surface fixes. In both the New Deal and the Marshall Plan, the solution was a broad range of actions. People were given jobs on public projects. Government and industry worked together on planning. Banks were encouraged to make certain kinds of investments. Individual consumers changed their habits.

It's easy to get discouraged about how much change is needed to battle the climate crisis, especially when we face so many other urgent crises, including racism and public health emergencies such as COVID-19. But these examples from history show us that when ambitious goals and strong policies come together, almost all aspects of a society can change to meet a common goal on a tight deadline.

The examples of the New Deal and the Marshall Plan show us something else. Each of them involved false starts, experiments, and course corrections along the way. The lesson from this is that we don't have to figure out every detail before we start. We can jump in and take action on a big, urgent project—such as a Green New Deal to fight climate change and bring about social justice.

But we can't do it if we don't start.

History has another lesson for us. It might be the most important of all. It is this: most of the changes that moved society toward greater sharing and fairness happened only because of one thing. That was the relentless pressure of large, organized groups of people. In other words, *movements*, such as the civil rights movement of the 1960s in the United States that ended legalized separation by race in schools and public life.

Movements will make, or break, the Green New Deal. Any presidents or governments that try to make a Green New Deal a reality will need powerful social movements backing them up, demanding change, and resisting efforts to hang on to harmful old ways. These movements will need to go beyond just supporting leaders and governments that steer their countries toward change—they will have to push those leaders and governments to do more. As Navarro Llanos said when urging a Marshall Plan for the Earth, we humans need to do something on a bigger scale than ever before.

We need to exercise our political power to campaign and vote for politicians who will fight for real climate action. But the big questions are not going to be settled by elections alone. Pressure from social and climate movements in the coming years will decide whether a Green New Deal pulls us back from the climate cliff.

Movements are groups of people who come together around two things. One is a shared goal or purpose, and the other is a determination to make their ideas heard, even if existing power structures try to drown them out or ignore them. A movement can be small—maybe three students who want to convince their school to create a pollinator garden to nourish bees and birds. It can be vast, like the waves of protest marches that fill city streets.

A movement can start out as small as a single Swedish schoolgirl sitting on a step, holding a sign that warns of climate change, then grow to cover the world.

CHAPTER 9

A TOOLKIT FOR YOUNG ACTIVISTS

Are you in school now? If so, you will be a young adult in 2030. By that time, the world should have cut its total carbon pollution by almost half. Just twenty years later, in 2050, carbon pollution should be down to zero.

As you've seen throughout this book, meeting this timetable gives us our best chance of keeping Earth's temperature from going up more than 1.5°C by the end of this century.

Decisions about whether or not we make those carbon cuts will shape your entire lives. Those decisions will be made before many of you are old enough to vote.

But through your actions today, you can keep reminding political leaders and candidates that you *will* vote someday soon. In the meantime, no one is too young to join the fight for a livable future.

The rest of this chapter has a number of suggestions for activism. Depending on how old you are, some of them will be more useful to you than others.

Maybe you're already doing one of the things in this chapter, or even more. If so, good for you! Every bit of activism helps, so you should feel empowered.

If you haven't yet found a path into activism, I hope one of these tools sounds like something you want to use. And because you are adventurous, open-minded, and creative, you may invent other ways to use these tools—or completely new tools!

CLIMATE CHANGE GOES TO SCHOOL

If you are a young person, chances are you spend a good amount of time in school. Does your school teach climate studies? For how long, and in what grades? Is climate change part of your earth science classes?

A study in the United Kingdom in 2018 showed that more than two thirds of students wanted to learn more at school about climate change and the environment. It also showed that about the same percentage of teachers wanted to do more teaching on those subjects. But many teachers didn't feel well prepared to teach them.

Now climate change education is becoming part of the school day in a number of countries. In 2019, Italy's top education official said that students in every grade would soon begin studying sustainability and climate change. The Southeast Asian nation of Cambodia also said that it is adding climate change to a new science curriculum for high school students.

In the United States, nineteen states and Washington, DC, have adopted the Next Generation Science Standards (NGSS). This program was introduced in 2013. It is a set of standards that spells out what students at various levels should be expected to know about science. The NGSS requires that climate change be taught as part of the science curriculum in the states that have adopted it. Students in middle school and high school, for example, would be taught about the connection between human activities and rising temperatures. They also learn about energy alternatives that produce less pollution than fossil fuels.

Twenty-one other states have adopted a different framework for teaching science from kindergarten through high school that also requires that schools teach climate change. You should be able to see your state's science standards on the state's official website or the website of the state education department.

If climate studies aren't taught at your school, or if you think more education on the subject is needed, find out who decides about your school's curriculum. In some cases, it is up to individual science teachers to decide how much climate science to teach, and how to teach it. In other cases, the school board of your school district, or your educational board, might make those decisions.

Once you know where the decisions are made, you could write a letter asking for more instruction on the climate, or start a petition for your fellow students to sign. You can also see if you can go to a Parent-Teacher Association or school board meeting to share your thoughts in person.

You'll find it helpful, whichever route you choose, to have a clear and specific statement of your goal. Be ready to explain what you are asking for, and why. You may find that other students—and their parents—want the same thing you want.

Also ask yourself, does your class or school ever have guest speakers? Ask your teacher or principal to look for speakers who can come to give presentations on environmental issues and climate change. What about field trips? If your school has such outings, do a little research on places you could suggest. Maybe there is a model solar-powered home in your area that gives demonstrations, or a wind-energy farm, or a science museum with an exhibit on climate change.

You can also focus your own schoolwork on climate change. If you are going to write a book report or create a science project, consider looking for a way to make it about climate change. It could be about the dangers, but it could also be about interesting solutions.

For shared projects, see if any of your classmates are willing to explore a topic that touches on climate change. Working on homework could spark conversations about climate change with your parents or friends. They may even help you find more research or ways to get involved.

MANY WAYS TO PROTEST

You've seen a lot of examples of climate protests in this book. For some people, protesting means joining a large, planned public march or gathering, such as a nationwide March for Science or Climate Strike. These events often bring together members of many organizations and movements. They also welcome individuals who don't identify with a particular group but want to stand up with those demanding action against pollution.

In big cities, these events can be huge. On the day of the Global Climate Strike in September 2019, a hundred thousand people marched in New York. Half a million marched in Montreal. But marches and demonstrations also took place in small towns and in the countryside. That same day, a group of nine researchers at a base in Antarctica stood in the snow, holding protest signs, to cheer and show support for the climate strikers worldwide.

In small communities, two dozen people marching down Main Street for the climate can be a big turnout. Their passion and concern are real, and it might take more bravery to march in a small group than in a large mass. After all, this problem is for all of us to solve, not just for the crowds that make news.

If a climate strike is scheduled for a school day and you want to take part, talk to your parents and teachers. Some schools now give all their students permission to be absent on those days. Some kids even go to marches or protest gatherings with their classmates and teachers. See if a teacher will make the protest march a school assignment—you could offer to write a paper about why climate activism matters to you, or a report after the march for your class or your school newspaper.

But marching in the streets is not the only kind of protest. Other methods have also brought about change.

One is making a statement by refusing to spend money on something.

People have boycotted products made by companies that are especially notorious polluters, or the banks that provide loans to them. People have also boycotted television shows that run ads from fossil-fuel companies. Boycotts become powerful when they spread through social media or letter-writing campaigns, so that thousands of people are telling a company or a network, "If you want our business, change your ways."

Pocketbook power works. According to the Yale Program on Climate Change Communication, boycotts by consumers have a bigger effect on corporations than most people realize. About a quarter of the boycotts that receive national attention succeed in changing corporations' practices. For example, because of pressure from the public for more humane treatment of orcas, Sea-World agreed to stop breeding these sea mammals in captivity. Boycotts and social media campaigns also led the company that owns Zara clothing stores to stop selling fur in a thousand locations.

Similar pressure can be put on the banks, insurance companies, and private investors that loan money to new fossil-fuel projects such as pipelines and fracking. With rallying cries such as #StopTheMoneyPipeline, activists are calling for these lenders to divest—withdraw their investments—from projects that harm the environment or make climate change worse, as we saw with Standing Rock. Banks and other lenders do not like to lose customers, so when activists say they will no longer do business with lenders who invest in fossil-fuel projects, the consequences are felt.

Divestment campaigns have made stock in fossil-fuel companies less attractive to many lenders and investors. Every big institution—like a university, a church, a foundation, or a city government—holds its money in some kind of fund or endowment. That money is then invested in stocks and bonds. It used to be that every major fund held investments in fossil-fuel companies. But thanks to the youth-led fossil-fuel-divestment movement, loosely coordinated by 350.org, funds totaling roughly $11 trillion have committed to eliminating their investments in fossil-fuel companies. And many of these funds have committed to investing in climate solutions instead.

You may not be a big investor with stock to divest from, but as a consumer you can still make a statement. You could stop buying food and beverages from stores that won't replace plastic straws and bags with recyclable paper ones. You could choose to eat a plant-based diet, because animal agriculture is a major contributor to climate change. You can buy books from local bookstores you can walk, bike, or bus to, or get books from your library, instead of ordering them from a faraway company that will burn energy shipping them to you.

And when you decide to join a protest march or demonstration, bring water in a reusable bottle. Individual acts of protest against waste and consumerism matter too. They matter even more if you can convince your whole school, or even your school board, to change what it buys and how it handles waste. If you've been reading about some of the young climate activists profiled in this book, you know that some of them successfully carried out campaigns to make their schools more green. See if you can convince your school to install solar panels on the roof, or start composting food waste. You may not be able to march in the nation's capital or even a state capital, but you're in school—so turn it into your arena for battling climate change.

Striking in the Global South

Before she graduated from high school, Vanessa Nakate became the first Fridays for Future climate striker in the African nation of Uganda. Her activism against climate change was spurred by concern for Uganda's people.

"I wanted to do something that would cause change to the lives of the people in my community and my country," Nakate says. "My country heavily depends on agriculture, therefore most of the people depend on agriculture. If our farms are destroyed by floods, if the farms are destroyed by droughts and crop production is less, that means that the price of food is going to go high. So it will only be the most privileged who will be able to buy food."

Vanessa Nakate organized the first Fridays for Future climate strike in Uganda.

As she researched ways to bring public attention to the problem, Nakate learned about the Fridays for Future climate strikes. Nakate decided to start by organizing four strikes. People did not know what to make of them. But Nakate learned a lesson that many activists have learned: that you can keep standing up for what you know is right, even if others mock or criticize you.

"Well, people found it very weird that I was on the streets," Nakate says. "And some of them threw some negative comments, like I was wasting my time, and the government will not listen to anything that I have to say. But I just kept going."

She kept going all the way to Madrid, Spain, where she joined climate protesters from around the world at a United Nations climate summit in 2019.

Nakate has been disappointed with the way the media covers climate change. She says, "They keep talking about climate change being a matter of the future, but they forget that [for] people of the Global South, it is a matter of now. And they have to help us report these things, because if they don't report these things, our leaders won't understand the importance of these strikes that we are holding."

Media, including social media, is essential to any movement today. For activists, this means two things. First, let your activism be based on good information from reliable sources. If you share incomplete or wrong information, it can end up hurting the cause you are trying to help. Second, if you agree with Nakate that important aspects of climate change are not being covered in the media you follow, you can write to newspapers, news networks, and other information sources to ask for broader coverage. Better yet, send a letter or petition signed by as many people as possible.

EXPLORE YOUR ENVIRONMENT

For some people, the path to activism is a hiking trail. Or a walk in a park, or a swim in a lake. Getting close to nature can lead to environmental activism.

Just spending time in nature *is* a form of activism. It says that the natural world matters, and that you care about it.

A small seed of environmental activism may grow into something big. Felix Finkbeiner was a fourth grader in Germany when he had to write a school paper on climate change. At first, he planned to write about saving his favorite animal. Then, as he says, "I realized it's not really about the polar bear, it's about saving humans."

While researching his paper, Finkbeiner read about African tree-planting activist Wangari Maathai. (See chapter 3 for more about Maathai.) He wrote the paper about what tree-planting can do to help the environment and fight climate change. When he presented it to his class, he ended it with a dramatic challenge: Germans should plant one million new trees in their country. A couple of months later, he planted his first tree. It was a small crab apple tree that his mother had bought for him to plant near the school. He later joked that if he had known how much attention it would get, he would have asked her for a more impressive tree.

News media and social media spread the word about the schoolkid who had made a stirring call for more trees. Finkbeiner's crusade received so much attention that, four years later, the United Nations invited him to New York to give a talk about tree-planting. By that time, Germany had planted its millionth tree.

Finkbeiner went on to start a nonprofit group called Plant-for-the-Planet. Its goal is a trillion new trees on Earth. The youth-focused group leads one-day workshops for children around the world. Kids learn how to plant trees and how to start their own tree-planting campaigns. As he has said, planting trees is something that kids can do to fight climate change now, without waiting for adults to solve the problem.

You don't have to make a speech at the United Nations or start an organization to share the benefits of planting trees. Remember, Finkbeiner's project started with just one tree. Look for parks in your area that are having tree-planting days and see if you can volunteer. Find out if an environmental organization, such as the Audubon Society or the Sierra Club, has a chapter close to you that is running a tree-planting project. Suggest a young people's tree-planting project for your school, camp, club, or religious organization.

Any tree-planting project, whether it's one new tree in your yard or a forest being restored, needs two things to succeed. First, the trees that are planted have to be the right ones for the location. They should be species that are native to the area, so that they can thrive in the local soil and weather. This is also good because native trees are ideal sources of food and habitat for the birds and animals that live in the area.

Second, trees have to be planted properly. This might mean digging the holes to a certain depth, or spacing them a certain distance apart. It might even mean that the young trees need fencing around them for the first few years, to protect them from nibbling animals. Nurseries that sell young trees for planting can give you this information. So can groups that organize planting projects.

There are many other ways to get close to nature. You might decide to take up camping or bird-watching. Try organic gardening as a way to learn about soil and the life cycles of plants. In a school garden, a yard, or a few pots on a windowsill or balcony, you can grow flowers or fresh herbs, greens, and vegetables.

Volunteering to be part of a cleanup crew is another form of outdoor activism. Many cities and local environmental groups sponsor "cleanup days," when groups of people gather trash from parks, trails, beaches, or stream banks.

Finally, a number of environmental organizations work around the world to protect the planet and its wildlife. Some of them welcome young members, and some of them sponsor hikes or volunteer projects in communities.

Do a little research and see if you can find a group that appeals to you. Teaming up with others may be your way to get green. It is also a reminder that the solution to climate change isn't just about the planet—it's also about the people we share it with.

"We Can't Eat Money, or Drink Oil"

Teenager Autumn Peltier is a water warrior. Peltier is a member of the Wiikwemikoong First Nation in Canada. Water has always been an important part of her life. Her home, an island in Ontario, is surrounded by the waters of Lake Huron.

When Peltier was eight years old, she visited

another First Nations community and was shocked to see a sign warning people not to drink the water without boiling it. This set her on the path of activism. She had a role model in her great-aunt Josephine Mandamin, who had devoted her life to protecting the waters of the Great Lakes—the five big bodies of water between Canada and the United States. Mandamin had once walked around all five lakes to call attention to water pollution.

Peltier began speaking up about the need for water protection. She was so vocal that at the age of fourteen, Peltier was named Chief Water Commissioner by the Anishinabek Nation—a post that her great-aunt had held before her death. This made Peltier the main spokesperson for water protection for forty First Nations in the province of Ontario. Peltier calls her great-aunt her hero. "I'm going to carry on her work until we don't have to anymore," she says.

Peltier has certainly carried on her great-aunt's work. She has spoken to Canada's prime minister and to gatherings at the United Nations about the right of all people to clean, safe water, and the importance of unpolluted water to the environment. She has called for a halt to industrial and commercial projects that harm or threaten people's water supplies. When she was fifteen, in 2019, she told a UN meeting, "I've said it once, and I'll say it again, we can't eat money, or drink oil." Her words are a reminder that even in wealthy nations, there are communities that do not have access to safe, healthy water. Usually those communities are where Black and Indigenous People live. One example in the United States is Flint, Michigan, where residents have battled for years against a failed water-management system and undrinkable water. Peltier's activism grows out of the principle that clean water should not be a privilege for some but a right for all.

GET POLITICAL

"We will mobilize to vote you out," said Komal Karishma Kumar. The young woman from the Pacific island nation of Fiji was speaking to United Nations officials in September 2019. She and other young climate activists were telling the leaders of member nations that kids are watching them. When they are old enough to vote, they will remember who took action to fight climate change, and who did not.

You may be a few years away from voting age, but

In a warning to "business as usual" political leaders, young climate activists show they want politics to change—and every day, more of them become voters.

you are not too young to get involved in politics. You will live the rest of your life in the world that today's political leaders are making with their actions on climate change—or their failures to act. It's not too early to start letting them know that you are paying attention.

If political action sounds to you like the best way to achieve social justice or fight climate change, start by finding out who your leaders are, from the local to the national level. What have they said about global warming and climate change? What have they said about the rights of the poor and of Indigenous People? Do their actions match their statements?

Consider going to town halls—meetings where your leaders answer questions and discuss issues with the community. If your leaders do not hold town halls, consider writing to them. If they have voted or taken action in ways that support fairness and fight climate change, thank them. If they haven't, explain what issue matters most to you, and why.

More and more politicians are beginning to realize that they need to start paying attention to young people. You may not yet be a voter, but you are a future voter. You may also have the power to influence how your older family members vote.

Speaking of voting, if you are old enough to vote in any election, do it. Research the candidates' positions. Support those that best represent your views and your hopes for the future. Volunteer to help with their campaigns.

The ultimate political activism is getting into politics yourself. If you thrive on the energy and excitement of politics, think about running for office. If there is a position you can compete for in your school or university, can you include an issue of social justice or climate change in your campaign? Your voice can inform or inspire others, to get more people involved in these issues.

Beyond school, voters in many parts of the world are electing young people to public office. Chlöe Swarbrick of New Zealand ran for office representing the Green Party, which takes strong positions in favor of protecting the environment and fighting climate change. She was elected to her country's parliament at the age of just twenty-three.

In Australia, voters elected Jordon Steele-John to the national parliament when he was twenty-two. The first elected member of parliament with a disability, Steele-John represents the Australian Greens, a party that supports ecological sustainability, social justice, and community-level democracy.

Steele-John has said that Australia should lower its voting age to sixteen, as some nations in Europe and South America have done. Hundreds of thousands of young people have already shown that they are focused on the future. Young people may also feel less pressure than adults to protect "business as usual" when it clearly isn't working. If sixteen-year-olds could vote in every country, would we be closer to a fair and livable climate future?

USE THE LAW

You've seen examples in this book about how young people are using the law to challenge governments, polluters, and pipeline developers. From climate-related complaints brought to the United Nations, to lawsuits against individual states and companies, legal actions will probably become more common as the climate crisis grows more urgent. Another one is unfolding now in the Pacific island nations.

Solomon Yeo and seven other law students from those nations founded an activist group called Pacific Islands Students Fighting Climate Change in 2019. The PISFCC is part of the Climate Action Network, an international collection of activist groups. The mission of the PISFCC is to fight climate change through legal means. It has asked the leaders of the Pacific island countries to pursue action on climate change at the United Nations and also at the International Court of Justice (ICJ).

"Firstly, climate change is threatening our fundamental human rights under international law, and secondly, we as Pacific Islanders must do everything we can to fight global carbon emissions," the group has said. Yeo hopes that bringing cases about climate change before the ICJ will "help states understand their duties to protect future generations."

Yeo and other young climate activists know that legal actions are generally time-consuming and can be costly. But, like politics and protest, the law is a tool that activists can use when the circumstances call for it.

You may find a way to add your support to an existing climate or justice lawsuit, like the young people who signed Zero Hour's petition in support of the kids who filed the *Juliana* lawsuit you read about in chapter 6. At some point you might even join with other like-minded young people to explore what it would take to start a climate lawsuit of your own. The law isn't always an easy tool to use, but it can be one of the most powerful.

GREEN ART

Creative people made historic works of art during the original New Deal. The government helped them as it helped other kinds of workers. Through the Works Progress Administration and the US Treasury, federal projects provided meaningful work for tens of thousands of painters, authors, musicians, playwrights, sculptors, filmmakers, actors, and craftspeople. Black and Indigenous artists received more support than they ever had before.

The result was an explosion of creativity. The Federal Art Project alone produced nearly 475,000 works of visual art, including 2,000 posters, 2,500 murals, and

100,000 paintings for public spaces. The Federal Music Project was responsible for 225,000 performances that reached a total of 150 million Americans.

Much of this art was simply about bringing joy and beauty to the lives of people during the misery of the Great Depression. Some artists, though, set out to capture that misery. They wanted to show why the New Deal was so desperately needed.

Today, as we face the fight to save our planet and each other, art can do the same things. It can both bring us joy and remind us what we're fighting for.

Warnings about climate change sometimes seem like a steady stream of terrible facts and images about how bad things are, or how much worse they could get. These facts and images have their place, but we also need pictures and songs and stories that give us hope. We need art that celebrates a positive future and how we can get there.

That is the spirit of the seven-minute animated film "A Message from the Future." You may have seen it in school. It has been shared in classrooms from the lower grades through universities. It is also available to watch online for free. I helped create the film, along with artist Molly Crabapple, Congresswoman Alexandria Ocasio-Cortez, filmmaker and climate justice organizer Avi Lewis (who also happens to be my husband), and more.

It's a story set in the future. It is about how, in the nick of time, enough people in the United States—the biggest economy on the planet—came to believe that we were worth saving. It shows the future built by a Green New Deal. Over lush paintings of a thriving world, Ocasio-Cortez speaks from the future, telling us what happened:

We changed how we did things. We became a society that was not only modern and wealthy but dignified and humane, too. By committing to universal rights like health care and meaningful work for all, we stopped being so scared of the future. We stopped being scared of each other. And we found our shared purpose.

As you'll see if you watch the film, one of the ways a "message from the future" can inspire activism in the present is by encouraging us to believe that change is possible, by helping us picture the world after we win.

Other artists are finding new ways to express their ideas about climate and justice. Environmental artist Xavier Cortada, who lives near Miami, painted numbers on thousands of signs, with wavy lines to mark the surface of the sea. He gave the signs to people who own homes in Pinecrest, outside Miami. Each homeowner's sign showed how much the water would have to rise to cover that property. A sign reading "3," for example, meant that a sea level rise of three feet would put that home underwater. Kids caught on and started painting similar signs and putting them along roads and near schools. This art project had an effect. A homeowners organization formed in Pinecrest to focus on climate change, with an ocean scientist as its leader.

Kids are creating climate art too. As you saw in chapter 3, a twelve-year-old girl wrote the song that school climate strikers sang in Christchurch, New Zealand. In Portland, Oregon, each year a project called Honoring Our Rivers invites students from kindergarten through college to create artwork, stories, and poems about the waterways of the region. Some of them are published in book form and presented to audiences at a bookstore. Libraries and other public buildings, as well as schools, often display posters and other artworks created by young people on environmental themes.

Maybe you are an artist, songwriter, or storyteller. Perhaps you are experimenting with creating films, video games, or comics. You can use any of these creative tools to share your thoughts, fears, hopes, and visions.

Creative people are always finding new ways to communicate. Knitters, for example, are now making "climate scarves." They look up the daily or yearly temperature records for their hometowns, their countries, or the world. They link the temperatures to colors, from dark blue for the coldest temperatures to dark purple for the hottest ones, with ranges of green, yellow, orange, and red in between. Then they knit long scarves. Each row stands for a day or year, with the color representing its temperature.

You can share your climate art in another way. If you have skills with a paintbrush or a sewing machine, offer to help your friends or classmates make signs, banners, or costumes to wear to marches and demonstrations. Art and protest often walk hand in hand. No matter what you choose, tap into your unique creativity. Art and entertainment can make people listen and help them understand a message, especially one that is difficult to hear.

FIND A MOVEMENT—OR START ONE

An activist working alone can still make a huge impact on the world.

Rachel Carson wasn't part of a movement when she wrote *Silent Spring*. But as you saw in chapter 5, her solitary, passionate work was a big inspiration for the environmental movement of the 1970s. And that movement, in turn, gave rise to a golden age of laws designed to protect the natural world.

More and more often, groups tackling a wide range of issues in social justice, environmentalism, and climate activism are merging their strengths in teaching events, projects, marches, and demonstrations. Both individual and group approaches are good. The road ahead has room for many causes and many kinds of activism.

If the idea of working with others for a common cause excites you, if you want to support and be supported by people who share your goals, then find a movement and jump in. Or create your own and see if others will jump in to join you.

Movements make a difference. You can be the friction, the resistance that is needed to slow down the machine that is setting the world on fire.

CONCLUSION
YOU ARE
THE THIRD FIRE

You are living through a turning point.

As you have seen throughout this book, humans face the potential for massive disaster brought about by climate change, but this dangerous moment in time also brings an extraordinary opportunity. We still have the power to save countless human lives, the landscapes we know, and many species of animals and plants.

The young organizers of the Sunrise Movement say that this moment is filled with both "promise and peril." The peril is climate breakdown, which is already under way. Certain people and parts of the world will suffer more than others, or sooner, but all of us are in peril—unless we limit our planet's warming. The *promise* is that we *can* limit that warming, if we are bold enough to seize the moment and make big changes. And in making those changes, we have the opportunity to address many other crises that our society faces, from homelessness to racism. The Green New Deal says: let's do it all at the same time!

Now is the time to rethink how we live, eat, travel, do business, and earn our livelihoods. Together we can do more than fight rising temperatures. The changes we make to protect the Earth can also protect and strengthen our most vulnerable and neglected communities, creating a safer and more just world for all.

Climate change makes all of our social ills worse. It speeds up or strengthens the bad effects of wars, racism, inequality, domestic violence, and lack of health care. What if, instead, it sped up or strengthened the forces that are working for peace, economic fairness, and social justice?

The climate crisis is a threat to the future of our species. The threat has a firm, science-based deadline. And this hard deadline might just be what we need to finally knit together movements that believe in the value of all people and the web of life.

Coming together in movements, hungry for environmental and social justice, young people like these marchers in Belgium—like you—can change the world.

Depending on what we do now, we can come out of this crisis with some things better than they were before. We can have renewable energy from sun and wind, as well as greener transportation and a world with more trees, wetlands, and grasslands. By protecting habitats and limiting our hunting of wildlife and the destruction of natural habitats, we can give the Earth's other species a better chance to live into the future with us. We'll have less waste because we will have lowered our use of plastic, especially disposable plastic, and we'll have cleaner air and water.

We can also have wider participation in government and planning, with more diverse voices. We can recognize the land rights of Indigenous Peoples and create opportunities to learn from their knowledge. We can have a world where wealth and resources are more fairly shared. We can refuse to treat any person or place as a "sacrifice zone."

Our house is on fire. It is too late to save *all* our stuff, but we can still save each other and a great many other species, too. Let's put out the flames and build something different in its place. Something a little less fancy, but with room for all those who need shelter and care.

I see three fires now. One fire is climate change, burning up the world we knew. Another fire is the rising anger, fear, and anti-immigrant sentiment that erupted in the New Zealand shooting you read about in chapter 3. These emotions are driving some political decisions around the world. They harden people's hearts and countries' borders against others, and they turn people toward authoritarian leaders.

But the third fire is the fire in the belly of the new generation of young activists like you. Your voices give us energy. Your visions point toward our best future. Now we have to feed that third fire and help it grow.

The more sparks the fire has, the brighter it will burn. I invite you to add your spark.

Are you ready to change everything?

LEARNING FROM THE CORONAVIRUS PANDEMIC

Just as I finished this book in the spring of 2020, a new, contagious virus appeared, infecting people with a disease known as COVID-19. It spread rapidly, and soon the world was in the grip of a coronavirus pandemic.

Millions of people were infected. Many lives were tragically lost, and families were shattered. The pandemic also cost people their jobs and businesses, drained resources such as food and medical supplies, and nearly shut down the economies of entire nations. Like the hurricanes, floods, and tornadoes that devastated

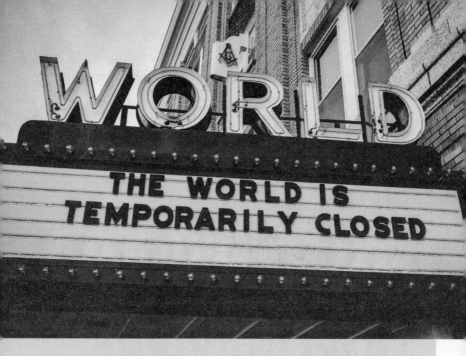

A coronavirus pandemic shut down the world (including a theater called the World) in early 2020. Like all disasters, it brought an opportunity for change.

communities you've read about throughout this book, the coronavirus was a disaster—one that unfolded on a global scale.

Now, as with those disasters, I invite you to think about the future, and about what the pandemic has shown us.

The coronavirus pandemic disrupted many of our existing systems, patterns, and ways of doing things. It is natural for people suffering through a disaster to yearn for a return to normality, but in reality, after such a big disaster, the world will not be the same. It will change—

but will the change be for the worse, or for the better?

Writing from India in the early months of the coronavirus crisis, author Arundhati Roy shared her vision of the pandemic as a portal—or doorway—to the future. She wrote: "Historically, pandemics have forced humans to break with the past and imagine their world anew. This one is no different. It is a portal, a gateway between one world and the next.

"We can choose to walk through it, dragging the carcasses of our prejudice and hatred, our avarice, our data banks and dead ideas, our dead rivers and smoky skies behind us. Or we can walk through lightly, with little luggage, ready to imagine another world. And ready to fight for it."

After this tragic crisis, in other words, we can scramble to get back to where we were, knowing that many people will be left behind. Or we can seize this chance to rebuild our future along different lines, with our concern widened to include everyone. As we think about how that future might be shaped, we should remember what we have learned during the pandemic, just as we must apply what we have learned about the climate crisis.

The pandemic revealed that many societies' leaders and agencies, the very things that were supposed to guide and help in a crisis, were poorly prepared, untrained,

As always happens during disasters, ordinary people found ways to help each other and their communities during the COVID-19 pandemic.

and unable to develop and communicate a clear plan for dealing with the virus. For years the public sphere had been starved of funds in the name of "small government." People with useful knowledge and experience had left or been removed from official positions. The result: when millions of people needed "big government" to help, they were left on their own, or were forced to rely on struggling local governments.

In the United States, with its high number of infections, the coronavirus highlighted what it means to have a medical system that is run for profit, rather than treating health care as every citizen's right. People without health insurance were afraid to seek treatment, while many who did seek treatment found the medical system unprepared to care properly for them. Hospital executives and leaders of the medical industry had long tried to spend as little money as possible and make as much as possible for themselves and their investors. They kept insisting on the fewest unfilled beds and the smallest staffs they could possibly get by on. They had never stockpiled the basic goods that would be needed in a public health emergency.

The virus isn't just an issue of public health, though. It also highlights many of the environmental truths explored in this book. In April 2020 a group of wildlife and ecosystem scientists with the Intergovernmental Science-Policy Platform on Biodiversity and Ecosystem Services wrote about the link between disease pandemics and our thoughtless use of nature. "Recent pandemics," they said, "are a direct consequence of human activity, particularly our global financial and economic systems that prize economic growth at any cost."

More than two thirds of new and emerging human diseases leap from animals to humans. The coronavirus, for example, is believed to have existed harmlessly in bats. But activities such as cutting down forests and creating mines, roads, and farms in formerly wild areas are bringing people into ever more contact and conflict with other species. So does exploiting wildlife for food and pets. And once a disease jumps from an animal into a human host, our crowded cities and global air travel help it spread quickly and widely among human populations. Plans for rebuilding economies after the coronavirus pandemic, the scientists said, must include stronger environmental protections around the world.

When governments acted to slow the spread of the virus by ordering businesses to close and people to work from home whenever possible, vehicle traffic fell to a fraction of its normal level. So did air travel. These changes seemed to bring good news for the climate: cleaner air and a reduction in greenhouse gas emissions. But positive though they were, these were short-term changes. They were forced on people, many of whom were eager to return to pre-pandemic "life as usual." These were not the long-term, thorough changes to our systems of energy and travel that are necessary to make cleaner air and lower emissions permanent.

Finally, the pandemic cast a cruel light on environmental injustice. Rates of serious illness and death were higher among people who lived in areas with high air pollution. Their bad environments had made them more vulnerable to the virus—and the people who lived in neighborhoods with the worst air pollution were often the poor and people of color. In this way, environmental injustice led to medical injustice.

After the crisis of the Great Depression in the 1930s, the United States found both the will and the money to transform society and lift up many suffering Americans. In times of crisis, ideas that once seemed impossible suddenly become possible—but which ideas? Sensible, fair ones designed to keep as many people as safe as possible, or predatory ideas designed to make the unimaginably rich even richer? Will the government spend billions of dollars to keep bailing out industries that are already wealthy, such as fossil fuels, cruise ships, and airlines? Or will that money instead be directed toward health care for all and toward a Green New Deal that will create jobs *and* fight climate change?

The biggest lesson I see from the coronavirus pandemic is that everyone, from individuals and families to government leaders, made difficult but necessary changes—changes none of us could have imagined before this. And many people rose to the challenge in creative and generous ways, making masks and equipment for health-care workers, checking on their elderly neighbors, doing what they could to help. Governments found funds to pump into their countries' economies.

The pandemic tested us in every way. It also showed us once again that big, rapid changes in society's direction are possible. It is possible, in fact, to Change Everything. Our challenge now is to use that creativity and energy, and those resources, not only against COVID-19 but also against climate change and injustice, and for a fairer future.

A NATURAL SOLUTION TO THE CLIMATE DISASTER

(PUBLIC LETTER OF APRIL 2019)

The world faces two existential crises, developing with terrifying speed: climate breakdown and ecological breakdown. Neither is being addressed with the urgency needed to prevent our life-support systems from spiralling into collapse. We are writing to champion a thrilling but neglected approach to averting climate chaos while defending the living world: natural climate solutions. This means drawing carbon dioxide out of the air by protecting and restoring ecosystems.

By defending, restoring and re-establishing forests, peatlands, mangroves, salt marshes, natural seabeds and other crucial ecosystems, large amounts of carbon can be removed from the air and stored. At the same time, the protection and restoration of these ecosystems can help minimise a sixth great extinction, while enhancing local people's resilience against climate disaster. Defending the living world and defending the climate are, in many cases, one and the same. This potential has so far been largely overlooked.

We call on governments to support natural climate solutions with an urgent programme of research, funding and political commitment. It is essential that they work with the guidance and free, prior and informed consent of Indigenous People and other local communities.

This approach should not be used as a substitute for the rapid and comprehensive decarbonisation of industrial economies. A committed and well-funded programme to address all the causes of climate chaos, including natural climate solutions, could help us hold the heating of the planet below 1.5C. We ask that they are deployed with the urgency these crises demand.

Greta Thunberg *Activist*
Margaret Atwood *Author*
Michael Mann *Distinguished professor of atmospheric science*
Naomi Klein *Author and campaigner*

Mohamed Nasheed *Former president, the Maldives*

Rowan Williams *former Archbishop of Canterbury*

Dia Mirza *Actor and UN environment goodwill ambassador*

Brian Eno *Musician and artist*

Philip Pullman *Author*

Bill McKibben *Author and campaigner*

Simon Lewis *Professor of global change science*

Hugh Fearnley-Whittingstall *Presenter and author*

Charlotte Wheeler *Forest restoration scientist*

David Suzuki *Scientist and author*

Anohni *Musician and artist*

Asha de Vos *Marine biologist*

Yeb Saño *Activist*

Bittu Sahgal *Founder, Sanctuary Nature Foundation*

John Sauven *Executive director, Greenpeace UK*

Craig Bennett *CEO, Friends of the Earth*

Ruth Davis *Deputy director of global programmes, RSPB*

Rebecca Wrigley *Chief executive, Rewilding Britain*

George Monbiot *Journalist*

FIND OUT MORE

Books

Diavolo, Lucy, ed. *No Planet B: A Teen Vogue Guide to the Climate Crisis*. Chicago: Haymarket Books, 2021.

Margolin, Jamie. *Youth to Power: Your Voice and How to Use It*. New York: Hachette Go, 2020.

Nardo, Don. *Planet Under Siege: Climate Change*. San Diego: Reference Point Press, 2020.

New York Times Editorial. *Climate Refugees*. New York: New York Times Educational Publishing, 2018.

Thunberg, Greta. *No One Is Too Small to Make a Difference*. New York: Penguin, 2019.

Online Resources to Help You Get Involved

https://www.youtube.com/watch?v=KAJsdgTPJpU
From PBS Newshour, Greta Thunberg's scorching speech at the United Nations on September 23, 2019.

https://www.youtube.com/watch?v=d9uTH0iprVQ
A Message from the Future
A short animated film about life after the Green New Deal, narrated by Alexandria Ocasio-Cortez, created by Molly Crabapple, Avi Lewis, and Naomi Klein.

https://www.youtube.com/watch?v=2m8YACFJlMg
A Message from the Future II: Years of Repair
This short animated film explores a future in which 2020's global pandemic and uprisings against racism became the springboard for a building a better society and healing our planet.

https://www.youtube.com/watch?v=_h1JbSBqZpQ
Autumn Peltier and Greta Thunberg
In this short film, Naomi Klein interviews young activists Autumn Peltier and Greta Thunberg, who were the subjects of documentaries at the Toronto International Film Festival in 2020.

https://solutions.thischangeseverything.org/
Beautiful Solutions brings together the stories, ideas, and values of environmental and social justice, with many examples of activists— including young people—working toward these goals around the world.

https://stopthemoneypipeline.com/
Stop the Money Pipeline is a movement that holds the fossil fuel industry accountable for the damage it is doing to our world's climate. Its works to educate people about the money behind fossil-fuel projects and to discourage banks and other institutions from investing in those projects.

https://leapmanifesto.org/en/the-leap-manifesto/
The Leap Manifesto is a call for energy democracy, social justice, and a public life "based on caring for the Earth and one another." Although Indigenous representatives and activists from many movements created The Leap as a plan for Canada, its vision applies everywhere.

https://www.youtube.com/watch?v=kP5nY8lzURQ
Sink or Swim is the 7.5-minute video of young activist Delaney Reynolds's TEDxYouth talk about climate change.

https://naomiklein.org/
Naomi Klein's website, with information about her journalism, books, and films.

https://www.sunrisemovement.org/
The website of the Sunrise Movement, where you can find online resources and information about groups in your area.

https://climatejusticealliance.org/workgroup/youth/
The webpage of the Youth Working Group of the Climate Justice Alliance.

https://www.earthguardians.org
Earth Guardians is committed to diversity and trains young people around the world to be leaders in the fight for environmental, climate, and social justice.

http://thisiszerohour.org
The website of Zero Hour, founded and led by activists of color.

https://strikewithus.org/
An anti-capitalist, working class, multiracial coalition of young people organizing for climate action.

https://www.vice.com/en_us/article/8xwvq3/11-young-climate-justice-activists-you-need-to-pay-attention-to-beyond-greta-thunberg
An online article with short profiles of some of the activists highlighted in this book, and others as well.

NOTES^{*}

Chapter 1: Kids Take Action

On Fire by Naomi Klein

https://www.theguardian.com/commentisfree/2019/sep/23/world
-leaders-generation-climate-breakdown-greta-thunberg

https://time.com/collection-post/5584902/greta-thunberg-next
-generation-leaders/

https://skepticalscience.com/animal-agriculture-meat-global-warming
.htm

https://unfoundation.org/blog/post/5-things-to-know-about-greta
-thunbergs-climate-lawsuit/

https://www.usatoday.com/story/news/world/2019/09/26/meet
-greta-thunberg-young-climate-activists-filed-complaint-united
-nations/2440431001/

https://earthjustice.org/blog/2019-september/greta-thunberg-young
-people-petition-UN-human-rights-climate-change/

* All links available as of April 29, 2020

Chapter 2: World Warmers

On Fire by Naomi Klein

This Changes Everything by Naomi Klein

https://www.newsweek.com/record-hit-ice-melt-antarctica-day-climate-emergency-1479326

https://www.theguardian.com/world/2019/dec/29/moscow-resorts-to-fake-snow-in-warmest-december-since-1886

https://www.theguardian.com/commentisfree/2019/dec/20/2019-has-been-a-year-of-climate-disaster-yet-still-our-leaders-procrastinate

https://www.vox.com/2019/12/30/21039298/40-celsius-australia-fires-2019-heatwave-climate-change

https://insideclimatenews.org/news/31102018/jet-stream-climate-change-study-extreme-weather-arctic-amplification-temperature

https://350.org/press-release/1-4-million-students-across-the-globe-demand-climate-action/

https://www.climate.gov/news-features/understanding-climate/climate-change-global-temperature

https://www.businessinsider.com/greenland-ice-melting-is-2070-worst-case-2019-8

https://www.ncdc.noaa.gov/news/what-paleoclimatology

https://www.giss.nasa.gov/research/features/201508_slushball

https://climate.nasa.gov/nasa_science/science/

https://nas-sites.org/americasclimatechoices/more-resources-on-climate-change/climate-change-lines-of-evidence-booklet/evidence-impacts-and-choices-figure-gallery/figure-9/

https://www.theguardian.com/environment/2019/nov/27/climate-emergency-world-may-have-crossed-tipping-points

https://www.ipcc.ch/sr15/chapter/spm/

https://insideclimatenews.org/news/19022019/arctic-bogs-permafrost-thaw-methane-climate-change-feedback-loop

https://www.climate.gov/news-features/understanding-climate/climate-change-global-sea-level

https://www.climate.gov/news-features/understanding-climate/climate-change-global-temperature

https://climateactiontracker.org/global/cat-thermometer/

https://www.ncdc.noaa.gov/sotc/global/201911

https://www.climaterealityproject.org/blog/why-15-degrees-danger-line-global-warming

https://www.reuters.com/article/us-palmoil-deforestation-study/palm-oil-to-blame-for-39-of-forest-loss-in-borneo-since-2000-study-idUSKBN1W41HD

https://oceanservice.noaa.gov/facts/acidification.html

https://www.npr.org/sections/thesalt/2018/06/19/616098095/as-carbon-dioxide-levels-rise-major-crops-are-losing-nutrients

https://climate.nasa.gov/evidence/

https://journals.ametsoc.org/doi/10.1175/BAMS-D-16-0007.1

https://earthobservatory.nasa.gov/features/GlobalWarming/page3.php

https://www.eia.gov/tools/faqs/faq.php?id=73&t=1

Chapter 3: Climate and Justice

The Shock Doctrine by Naomi Klein

No Is Not Enough by Naomi Klein

This Changes Everything by Naomi Klein

"Only a Green New Deal Can Douse the Fires of Eco-Fascism" (https://theintercept.com/2019/09/16/climate-change-immigration-mass-shootings/) by Naomi Klein

https://www.greenpeace.org.uk/news/black-history-month-young-climate-activists-in-africa/

https://www.nobelprize.org/prizes/peace/2004/maathai/biographical/

https://www.bloomberg.com/graphics/2019-can-renewable-energy-power-the-world/

https://wagingnonviolence.org/2016/03/how-montanans-stopped-otter-creek-mine-coal-in-north-america/

https://theintercept.com/2019/09/16/climate-change-immigration-mass-shootings/

https://www.huffpost.com/entry/naomi-klein-climate-green-new-deal_n_5e0f66e4e4b0b2520d20b7a5

https://lareviewofbooks.org/article/against-climate-barbarism-a-conversation-with-naomi-klein/

https://theintercept.com/2019/09/16/climate-change-immigration-mass-shootings/

https://www.huffpost.com/entry/naomi-klein-climate-green-new-deal_n_5e0f66e4e4b0b2520d20b7a5

https://lareviewofbooks.org/article/against-climate-barbarism-a-conversation-with-naomi-klein/

https://www.theguardian.com/environment/2016/oct/26/oil-drilling-underway-beneath-ecuadors-yasuni-national-park

https://news.mongabay.com/2019/07/heart-of-ecuadors-yasuni-home-to-uncontacted-tribes-opens-for-oil-drilling/

Chapter 4: Burning the Past, Cooking the Future

This Changes Everything by Naomi Klein

https://www.egr.msu.edu/~lira/supp/steam/wattbio.html

http://ipod-ngsta.test.nationalgeographic.org/thisday/dec4/great-smog-1952/

https://www.history.com/news/the-killer-fog-that-blanketed-london-60-years-ago

https://www.usatoday.com/story/news/world/2016/12/13/scientists-say-theyve-solved-mystery-1952-london-killer-fog/95375738/

https://theculturetrip.com/europe/united-kingdom/england/london/articles/london-fog-the-biography/

Chapter 5: The Battle Takes Shape

This Changes Everything by Naomi Klein

On Fire by Naomi Klein

https://www.teenvogue.com/gallery/8-young-environmentalists -working-to-save-earth

https://www.sanclementetimes.com/ground-san-clemente-high-school -environmental-club-gets-ready-new-year/

https://acespace.org/people/celeste-tinajero/

http://miamisearise.com/

https://www.scientificamerican.com/article/exxon-knew-about-climate -change-almost-40-years-ago/

https://www.theguardian.com/commentisfree/2020/jan/20/big-oil -congress-climate-change

https://thebulletin.org/2019/12/fossil-fuel-companies-claim-theyre -helping-fight-climate-change-the-reality-is-different/

https://insideclimatenews.org/content/Exxon-The-Road-Not-Taken

https://www.ucsusa.org/sites/default/files/attach/2015/07/The-Climate -Deception-Dossiers.pdf

https://www.thenation.com/article/exxon-lawsuit-climate-change/

https://www.bloomberg.com/news/articles/2019-09-12/houston-ship -channel-partially-shut-by-greepeace-protestors

https://www.greenpeace.org/usa/meet-the-brave-activists-who-shut -down-the-largest-fossil-fuel-ship-channel-in-the-us-for-18-hours/

https://www.theguardian.com/us-news/2019/nov/23/harvard-yale -football-game-protest-fossil-fuels

https://www.theguardian.com/business/2020/jan/15/harvard-law -students-protest-firm-representing-exxon-climate-lawsuit

https://www.independent.co.uk/news/uk/home-news/extinction -rebellion-shell-aberdeen-protest-climate-crisis-xr-a9286331.html

Chapter 6: Protecting Their Homes—and the Planet

This Changes Everything by Naomi Klein

https://www.cbc.ca/news/business/enbridge-northern-gateway
-agm-1.512878

http://priceofoil.org/2016/07/01/victory-for-first-nations-in-northern
-gateway-fight/

https://insideclimatenews.org/news/03052018/enbridge-fined-tar
-sands-oil-pipeline-inspections-kalamazoo-michigan-dilbit-spill

https://www.cer-rec.gc.ca/sftnvrnmnt/sft/dshbrd/dshbrd-eng.html

https://www.npr.org/2018/11/29/671701019/2-years-after-standing
-rock-protests-north-dakota-oil-business-is-booming

https://psmag.com/magazine/standing-rock-still-rising

https://theintercept.com/2017/05/27/leaked-documents-reveal-security
-firms-counterterrorism-tactics-at-standing-rock-to-defeat-pipeline
-insurgencies/

https://www.nytimes.com/interactive/2016/11/23/us/dakota-access
-pipeline-protest-map.html

https://theintercept.com/2017/05/27/leaked-documents-reveal-security
-firms-counterterrorism-tactics-at-standing-rock-to-defeat-pipeline
-insurgencies/

https://www.phmsa.dot.gov/

https://earther.gizmodo.com/this-14-year-old-standing-rock-activist
-got-a-spotlight-1823522166

https://www.billboard.com/articles/events/oscars/8231872/2018-oscars
-andra-day-common-marshall-performance-activists-who-are-they

https://www.ourchildrenstrust.org/juliana-v-us

https://static1.squarespace.com/static/571d109b04426270152febe0
/t/5e22508873d1bc4c30fad90d/1579307146820
/Juliana+Press+Release+1-17-20.pdf

https://www.theatlantic.com/science/archive/2020/01/read-fiery-dissent
-childrens-climate-case/605296/

https://time.com/5767438/climate-lawsuit-kids/

https://www.businessinsider.com/juliana-vs-united-states-kids-climate
-change-case-dismissed-2020-1

http://ourislandsourhome.com.au/

https://www.theguardian.com/australia-news/2019/may/13/torres-strait
-islanders-take-climate-change-complaint-to-the-united-nations

https://www.businessinsider.com/torres-strait-islanders-file-un-climate
-change-complaint-against-australian-government-2019-5

Chapter 7: Changing the Future

This Changes Everything by Naomi Klein

On Fire by Naomi Klein

The Battle for Paradise by Naomi Klein

https://www.theguardian.com/environment/2019/apr/03/a-natural
-solution-to-the-climate-disaster

https://www.globalccsinstitute.com/resources/global-status-report/

https://www.virgin.com/content/virgin-earth-challenge-0

https://www.sciencedirect.com/science/article/pii/S1876610217317174

https://blogs.ei.columbia.edu/2018/11/27/carbon-dioxide-removal
-climate-change/

https://www.treehugger.com/environmental-policy/environmentalists
-call-carbon-capture-and-storage-forests.html

https://www.ipcc.ch/sr15/

https://www.themanufacturer.com/articles/carbon-capture-and
-storeage-takes-a-step-forward/

https://horizon-magazine.eu/article/storing-co2-underground-can
-curb-carbon-emissions-it-safe.htm

https://www.nationalgeographic.com/environment/2019/07/how-to
-erase-100-years-carbon-emissions-plant-trees/

https://www.bgs.ac.uk/science/CO2/home.html

https://science.sciencemag.org/content/365/6448/76

https://www.technologyreview.com/s/614025/geoengineering-experiment-harvard-creates-governance-committee-climate-change/

https://www.scientificamerican.com/article/risks-of-controversial-geoengineering-approach-may-be-overstated/

https://www.iflscience.com/environment/bill-gatesbacked-controversial-geoengineering-test-moves-forward-with-new-committee/

https://www.salon.com/2020/01/14/why-solve-climate-change-when-you-can-monetize-it/

https://www.nationalgeographic.com/environment/oceans/dead-zones/

https://www.sciencedaily.com/releases/2012/06/120606092715.htm

https://www.businessinsider.com/elon-musk-spacex-mars-plan-timeline-2018-10

https://www.popularmechanics.com/science/a30629428/rand-paul-climate-change-terraform-planets/

https://www.vice.com/en_us/article/8xwvq3/11-young-climate-justice-activists-you-need-to-pay-attention-to-beyond-greta-thunberg

https://www.umass.edu/events/workshop-student-leadership

https://solutions.thischangeseverything.org/module/rebuilding-greensburg,-kansas

https://www.usatoday.com/story/news/greenhouse/2013/04/13/greensburg-kansas/2078901/

https://www.kshs.org/kansapedia/greensburg-tornado-2007/17226

https://www.kansas.com/news/weather/tornado/article147226009.html

https://www.kwch.com/content/news/Greensburg--420842963.html

https://www.usgbc.org/articles/rebuilding-and-resiliency-leed-greensburg-kansas

Chapter 8: A Green New Deal

On Fire by Naomi Klein

This Changes Everything by Naomi Klein

https://web.stanford.edu/class/e297c/poverty_prejudice/soc_sec/hgreat.htm

https://www.theatlantic.com/ideas/archive/2019/03/surprising-truth
-about-roosevelts-new-deal/584209/

https://www2.gwu.edu/~erpapers/teachinger/glossary/nya.cfm

https://livingnewdeal.org/creators/national-youth-administration/

https://history.state.gov/milestones/1945-1952/marshall-plan

https://solutions.thischangeseverything.org/module/buen-vivir

https://www.theguardian.com/sustainable-business/blog/buen-vivir
-philosophy-south-america-eduardo-gudynas

https://www.history.com/topics/great-depression/civilian-conservation
-corps

Chapter 9: A Toolkit for Young Activists

On Fire by Naomi Klein

https://www.campaigncc.org/schoolresources

https://edsource.org/2019/teachers-and-students-push-for-climate
-change-education-in-california/618239

https://www.scientificamerican.com/article/some-states-still-lag-in
-teaching-climate-science/

https://www.studyinternational.com/news/climate-change-education
-schools/

https://www.nytimes.com/2019/11/05/world/europe/italy-schools
-climate-change.html

https://www.nbcnews.com/news/world/global-climate-strike-protests
-expected-draw-millions-n1056231

https://www.buzzfeednews.com/article/zahrahirji/climate-strike-greta
-thunberg-fridays-for-future

https://climatecommunication.yale.edu/publications/consumer
-activism-global-warming/

https://www.commondreams.org/news/2020/02/03/divestment-fever-spreads-eco-radicals-goldman-sachs-downgrade-exxon-stock-sell

https://350.org/press-release/global-fossil-fuel-divestment-11t/

https://www.democracynow.org/2019/12/12/cop25_vanessa_nakate_uganda

https://www.nationalgeographic.com/news/2017/03/felix-finkbeiner-plant-for-the-planet-one-trillion-trees/

https://www.plant-for-the-planet.org/en/home

https://www.reuters.com/article/us-climate-change-un-youth/young-climate-activists-seek-step-up-from-streets-to-political-table-idUSKBN1W60OD

https://www.businessinsider.com/youngest-politicians-around-world-2019-3#senator-jordon-steele-john-elected-in-2017-at-the-age-of-22-is-currently-the-youngest-member-of-australias-parliament-he-is-also-the-first-with-a-disability

https://www.reuters.com/article/us-climate-change-un-youth/young-climate-activists-seek-step-up-from-streets-to-political-table-idUSKBN1W60OD

http://www.wansolwaranews.com/2019/08/09/law-students-push-for-urgent-advisory-opinion-as-climate-fight-gains-momentum/

http://www.sciencenewsforstudents.org/article/using-art-show-climate-change-threat

https://willamettepartnership.org/honoring-our-rivers-fledges-the-nest/

Conclusion: You Are the Third Fire

On Fire by Naomi Klein

This Changes Everything by Naomi Klein

PHOTO CREDITS

ACKNOWLEDGMENTS

Naomi:

What a joy it has been to find such a dedicated and talented collaborator in Rebecca Stefoff. Her vision and careful labor made this book possible, and she wrote many of the inspiring profiles of young climate activists found in its pages. Boundless thanks to Anthony Arnove for pairing us up and for making this project happen. Alexa Pastor created a wonderful publishing home for us and offered many helpful editorial insights. Rajiv Sicora lent his prodigious climate knowledge to the fact-check, Jackie Joiner conducted us all with unflagging focus and grace, and Avi Lewis is my partner in all things. This book draws on a decade and a half of research and writing, which means I have no hope of acknowledging all of the scientists, activists, fellow writers, editors, agents, and friends whose support makes my work possible. Instead, I would like to thank the young readers whose curiosity, morality and love for the natural world bring joy and inspiration to life: Zoe, Aaron, Theo, Zev, Yoav, Zimri, Yoshi, Mika, Tillie, Levi, Nate, Eve, Arlo, Georgia, Miriam, Beatrice, Mavis, Leo, Nick, Adam, and, of course, our beautiful ocean boy, Toma.

Rebecca:

I am deeply grateful to Naomi Klein and Anthony Arnove for making me a part of this book—and to Naomi for her inspiring work over many years. Many thanks are due also to the teams at Atheneum Books for Young Readers and elsewhere who helped hone the book and put it out into the world, and to my invariably supportive partner, Zachary Edmonson. Above all, I am immeasurably grateful for the passion of young activists everywhere: those who are already working to change everything, and those who are yet to come.

NAOMI KLEIN is an award-winning journalist, columnist, documentary filmmaker, and author of the *New York Times* and international bestsellers *The Shock Doctrine*, *No Logo*, *This Changes Everything*, *No Is Not Enough*, and *On Fire*. Her writing has appeared in newspapers and magazines around the world, and she is senior correspondent for *The Intercept*. Klein is the inaugural Gloria Steinem Endowed Chair in Media, Culture and Feminist Studies at Rutgers University and cofounder of the climate justice organization The Leap (TheLeap.org).

REBECCA STEFOFF published her first books when she was in college and has been writing ever since. She has written many nonfiction books for children and young adults, with an emphasis on science and history, including a young readers adaptation of Darwin's *On the Origin of Species*. Through her books, teenage readers can explore topics as varied as ghosts, robots, bacteria, evolution, women pioneers, the ruins of Great Zimbabwe, forensic crime solving, and more. She lives in Portland, Oregon.